WORLD
CRICKET

Publisher's Note

Donald Woods, born in Transkei, Cape Province, South Africa, was until late 1977
the only white member of the 17-man Governing Council of the South African
Cricket Board of Control. In this capacity he was working as an intermediary between
the non-racial body on the one hand, and the all-white South African Cricket
Association and the South African Government's Ministry of Sport on the other, to
try and reach a negotiated settlement removing apartheid from South African cricket.
But on October 19, 1977, he was arrested by the South African Security Police and
subjected to banning orders which imposed a form of house arrest, following his
protests against the death in Security Police Custody of his friend Steve Biko, leader
of the Black Consciousness Movement.
Three months later he escaped with his family across the border into Lesotho and via
Zambia to London, where they have since lived. The account of this escape was
portrayed in Sir Richard Attenborough's film *Cry Freedom*, in which the author's
concerns about South Aftican sport were also depicted.
Donald Woods works as a writer, lecturer and broadcaster on South African affairs.
In addition to his cricket administration in South Africa, he was at the time of his
arrest also a member of the non-racial South African Rugby Union, and was South
Africa's delegate to the International Chess Federation.
Donald Wood's passion for cricket, and his special knowledge of the background to
South Africa's exclusion from world cricket which was dramatically ended in 1992,
gives this personal account of the 1992 World Cup a poignant and unique validity.

WORLD CRICKET

REFLECTIONS ON THE 1992 WORLD CUP

DONALD WOODS

with contributions from

Qamar Ahmed, Mihir Bose, Hugh Crosskill,
Ralph Dellor, Iain Galloway, Brian Johnston,
Bob Nixon, Neville Oliver, Vijay Rana

Acknowledgements

Special thanks are due to Derek Wyatt for first backing the notion of this book; to David Frith, Editor of *Wisden Cricket Monthly* magazine for his encouragement throughout; to Mike Popham of the BBC World Service for promoting it to the stage of its acceptance by Broadcast Books, and to Alastair Lack of the World Service for his enthusiastic support. The painstaking task of co-ordinating contribution from crickeet writers around the world, and of checking the final manuscript was zlso done by Mike Popham, and by Chris Florence of the World Service Sports department.

Thanks are also due to Ali Bacher, Steve Tshwete, Mike Proctor, Neil Adcock, Trevor Chesterfield, Anthony Lewis and Sir Colin Cowdrey for enjoyable times and talks during the weeks of the World Cup in Australia and New Zealand, which helped me considerably in the writing of the match accounts and general comments.

And final but no less heartfelt thanks must go to Dr Tom Mason for his skillful editorship of the manuscript and to Steve Dobell for his scorecard compilations.

I am deeply grateful to all the above-named for helping to make this book a reality, and I hope readers have even half the fun reading it that I had in writing it!

Donald Woods
LONDON 1992

Broadcast Books
4 Cotham Vale
Bristol BS5 6HR

©1992 BBC World Service

ISBN 1874092 03 6

Designed by Oliver Hickey
and Carl Meek

Cover Photograph: Patrick Eagar

Printed and bound in Great Britain by
The Bath Press, Avon

Contents

For my son, Dillon Woods,
who has fortunately inherited the cricket virus.

Prologue

Thoughts Home and Away

IN 1992 I *fulfilled a long-held ambition – to take a month off from all other aspects of life and do nothing but watch international cricket. The 1992 World Cup being staged in Australia and New Zealand, I secured journalistic commissions to cover the costs, and set off happily for the Antipodes, scarcely believing I would soon actually be at such famous stadiums as Woolloongabba ("The Gabba") in Brisbane, the Sydney Cricket Ground and the giant 108,000-seater in Melbourne, not to mention the Adelaide Oval, Eden Park in Auckland, Lancaster Park in Christchurch and the Basin Reserve in Wellington.*

All my life I had been reading of such places, and the great deeds done there over more than a century by the heroes of cricketing history. As I packed I included a copy of Wisden in the spirit of one who wouldn't dream of setting off on a pilgrimage without the Bible.

My three sons understood my excitement completely, but my wife and two daughters – though no less pleased for my sake – found the attractions of the venture as incomprehensible as I find those of mountaineering, potholing, horse-racing and having to go to the dentist. Not that my wife, Wendy, is anti-cricket. In fact, it was at a Test Match that I first fully began to realise the extent to which I was attracted to her. She was sixteen. I was twenty-three. Neil Adcock was bowling to Colin Cowdrey for South Africa against England at Kingsmead, Durban, in January 1957, and there she was with her parents – unbored. She even overheard, and remembered, something a perspiring Brian Statham said in regretfully declining a beer from the crowd while fielding on the boundary: "Ehh – it wouldn't tooch sides!"

After thirty years of marriage I now realise that this constituted somewhat less than a lifelong obsession with cricket on her part. Yet I have to say she is generally less bored by cricket than by other sports. She says her heart sinks when she enters a room with a television screen showing expanses of green, but I think she means more those expanses of green which depress me as well – relating to horse-racing, show-jumping, sheepdog trials and less-than-highest-class soccer attended by wailing crowds singing dirge-like songs very badly. Personally I find those particularly depressing expanses of televised green joyfully outweighed by those delightful expanses of green related to rugby, golf, Wimbledon tennis and, above all and in particular, the astonishing variety of world cricket.

The endless variety of cricket is typified by the various pronunciations of the word. Richie Benaud and many Australians call it Crikkut; *the New Zealanders call it* Cruckutt; *Dr. Ali Bacher and many South Africans in the Transvaal region call it* Crigged *and Geoffrey Boycott, perhaps uniquely, calls it* Creek Eat. *My wife calls it something else entirely when she bounds into the room to watch a favourite programme and sees the stumps, the pitch and the green outfield filling the screen – this in spite of that memorable day long ago at the Kingsmead Test Match ...*

Actually it was an engrossing contest, that match, in which South Africa led England on the first innings thanks to a swashbuckling century by my special hero, Roy McLean, and in spite of what struck me as the unspeakably negative batting and bowling of Trevor Bailey. Denis Compton, Peter May, Colin Cowdrey – these were great players, but Bailey was, I always thought, a blight upon the game. His bat had an anaesthetic effect on spectator interest and his bowling was so wide of the leg stump that, on one occasion, McLean ostentatiously pointed out to him where the stumps were.

It is characteristic of the English – a fairly masochistic people – that they still speak of the few matches Bailey

saved for England. They never speak of the many which slow batting by Bailey – or by Boycott or Tavaré, for that matter – surely cost England all hope of winning.

That Kingsmead match in 1957 was saved for England by a century from Doug Insole, but it had been one of the most engrossing contests in a close-fought series which was ultimately shared two Tests all. It also produced one of my favourite lines in all cricket-writing, when Alan Ross described how Johnny Wardle bowled the big tail-end batsman Peter Heine with a left-handed googly. The "Chinaman" from Wardle to Heine, wrote Ross, "was as an epigram from Herodotus to a simple tiller of the soil, and the stumps sagged".

Does any other game inspire such refined enthusiasm – or such writing? Surely no other physical sport even approaches the volume of literature produced on cricket, running into many hundreds of books with dozens more being produced every year. And the standard of the top writing is so high that there is now a select pantheon of the cricket-writing immortals over the past century led by Neville Cardus, R.C. Robertson-Glasgow, Ian Peebles, E. W. Swanton, John Arlott and Alan Ross from England; Ray Robinson, Arthur Mailey and Jack Fingleton from Australia and C.L.R. James from the West Indies.

These writers not only covered cricket, they produced literature in the process. Just as Chopin's études, composed primarily as technical keyboard exercises, became artistic classics, so the work of these writers elevated cricket reporting to new heights and added new dimensions to the culture of the world game.

The cricket commentator, Ralph Dellor, once knew a journalist who gave up the job of cricket correspondent for a national newspaper because he felt it was, geographically, too restrictive:

> It was a wonderful life, reporting on cricket from places like Australia and the West Indies, but there were so many other parts that I would not have got to had I confined my professional activities to cricket.

Dellor took it that the correspondent must have been talking about other parts of the universe rather than other parts of the world: "for there appears to be not a corner of the globe that has not staged a game of cricket at some time or another. Had it been two Englishmen who had set foot on the Moon in July 1969 you could have been pretty certain that they would have started an impromptu game of cricket. Everybody knows about the cricket played in those countries which are full members of the International Cricket Council – the Test-playing nations. Even casual followers will know that the game is played elsewhere. Not many will realise that you can go through the alphabet from Argentina to Zambia and find organised cricket. How many, for instance, appreciate that there is a cricket club in Japan? Members of the MCC might think that they belong to an exclusive organisation, but to belong to the Yokahama Cricket Club – now that is exclusive."

It may be that cricket will turn out to be the most enduring legacy of the British Empire. It seems to have a strange appeal for so many who have no reason to be grateful to their one-time rulers. Ralph Dellor used to be told in school history lessons that "trade follows the flag" – "meaning that commercial concerns followed the army into numerous areas of the world during the eighteenth and nineteenth centuries. Like many a neat phrase, it was then proved to be slightly inaccurate in that the flag often followed trade. There were occasions when the army was sent in to convince doubting locals that they really did want to conduct business with the British. But whether it was business or battles which took the British overseas, it was certain that following close at hand would be cricket. As there were few areas of the world which did not receive a visit of one kind or the other at some stage in development, so the seed of cricket was scattered widely. For mysterious reasons, in some places it flourished and in others withered as a quaint anachronism in the local landscape."

Cricket having been played for more than three hundred years, and having evolved through various stages of development covering many generations in the many countries, it is no wonder that there have been so many books on this one extraordinary game.

Well, this is yet another cricket book.

A disputed decision between two young cricketers in Bombay.

The joy of cricket in the outer suburbs of Lahore.

It should be unlike most of the others in that it certainly isn't written by a famous player, nor even by a cricket writer – though the book draws on the words of a team of commentators put together by the BBC World Service: Qamar Ahmed on Pakistan, Mihir Bose on India, Hugh Crosskill on the West Indies, Ralph Dellor on cricketing 'minor countries', Iain Gallaway on New Zealand, Brian Johnston on England, Bob Nixon on Zimbabwe, Neville Oliver on Australia and Vijay Rana on Sri Lanka. This book might interest most cricket fans because it is written by one of them – by one of that vast army of Those-Who-Didn't-Make-It-Into-Test-Cricket-But-Love-The-Game-Anyway.

We are many and we are as one. We are those who realised one day, probably after being driven for the fourth four in one over or after being dismissed for a paltry few yet again when well set, that we were, after all, not going to make it to international level. We have, at various times, had our Moments with bat or ball which had given rise to secret, and sometimes not-so-secret, hopes of one day emulating our heroes and walking out to bat at Lords, or pacing out our twenty-yard run-up to the wicket while absent-mindedly polishing the ball, seemingly oblivious of the excited thousands in the stands. But then, barely in our twenties, has come the final acknowledgment that this was not to be – followed by a further realisation that not only would we never become Test cricketers but that, further, we were among the Mortal Majority to whom a fast ball from a fast bowler actually travels fast.

To your Bradmans and Headleys and Hammonds, as to your Gowers, Boons and Crowes, that doesn't happen. Where we see a flashing sphere hurtling towards us, they see a slow, floating balloon coming down the pitch so deliberately that they have time to place their feet in exactly the right position, look around to decide which gap in the field to penetrate, then unwind an elegant stroke which transforms the slow, soft balloon into a hard leather cricket ball rocketing towards the boundary.

Along with my interest as a not-quite-player I had another interest in this World Cup, partly political, partly sentimental. I was born in South Africa and have felt involved with South African cricket since childhood. I expected South Africa to field a team quite capable of winning the World Cup and certainly of reaching at least the semi-final stage. Above all, the presence in this tournament of a team from South Africa completed again the international cricket family, making the 1992 World Cup the most representative in history – a World Cup indeed.

Many will remember how Basil D'Oliiveira, born in Cape Town and officially classified as "coloured" (of mixed race) barred under the apartheid laws from playing cricket for his own country, was helped by John Arlott to play county cricket in England and was chosen to tour South Africa with the England team of 1968-1969; and of how the South African government prohibited the tour because of this, resulting in the world-wide boycott of South African cricket by the official bodies of all the major cricketing countries which had lasted for twenty-two years — twenty-two years of isolation that were now coming to an end.

Filled with all these thoughts on the beauties and complexities of cricket, on its history, its many dimensions and its wide following in the world, I revelled in the prospect of seeing teams from England, Australia, West Indies, India, Pakistan, South Africa, New Zealand, Sri Lanka and Zimbabwe competing for the world crown. These national teams, after all, contained players who had attained the rank of that wonderful few competing at international level, and they would be performing for the admiring many who never made it. Among these few were exceptional stars already established, such as the teenage genius Sachin Tendulkar of India, and the tournament would inevitably reveal others of exceptional talent as yet unsung but soon to be household names.

And I would be there to watch and witness!

So in admiration of the wonderful few, on behalf of the admiring many, I set off to cover the 1992 World Cup and to write this book about it.

Donald Woods
LONDON, 1992

A view from the new stand at Melbourne.

Reflections en Route

Alien Territories

I had to go via the United States, where I had some lectures to deliver on the South African situation, and so en route to Sydney via New York, Washington, Chicago, San Francisco and Los Angeles I had time to ponder the significance of this 1992 World Cup over its predecessors.

It would be the fifth and the most representative, now with South Africa back in the fold, and it would probably have a new winner. The first two World Cup tournaments, held in England in 1975 and 1979, had been won by the West Indies, and the third in 1983, also held in England, had been won by India. The fourth, held in 1987 in India and Pakistan, had been won by Australia.

> In 1975 West Indies had beaten Australia in the final at Lord's.
> In 1979 West Indies had beaten England in the final at Lord's.
> In 1983 India had beaten West Indies in the final at Lord's.
> In 1987 Australia had beaten England in the final at Calcutta.

This time England, twice runners-up for the title, were favoured by most critics to win, having a powerful team with great depth in batting and a well-balanced bowling attack.

- South Africa were the unknown quantity, having been out of international cricket for twenty-two years because of the apartheid policy.
- Australia, the holders of the title, were joint favourites with England in most of the betting-shops or seeded second among the cognoscenti.
- West Indies were expected to reach at least the semi-final stage if not actually to win, but were no longer quite as dreaded by opponents as in the recent past.
- Pakistan were highly regarded, but not quite as highly as they had been before it was known that the electrifying young fast bowler, Waqar Younis, was injured and would be unable to play.
- India were also known to be a powerful team, but had had a gruelling recent itinerary of matches, as had Australia.

It was my view, as I travelled across America, that the winner of the 1992 World Cup would be one of these six teams – England, Australia, West Indies, Pakistan, India or South Africa. I couldn't realistically see Sri Lanka, Zimbabwe or New Zealand taking the title. Subsequent events were to shake the confidence with which I had decided this, but at that stage that was how things looked to me. So much for the study of form in team sport, and especially the less-than- predictable sport of cricket!

"Cricket, huh?" said my lecture agent Carlton Sedgeley in his Manhattan office, his honest brow frowning as he tried to understand why I would journey to the other side of the world, literally, for "a kind of baseball, I guess, only played with a sorta paddle, right?"

"Not really," I said, pointing out that when we in cricket spoke of a world series we meant it – a real world series contested initially by dozens of national teams and ultimately by nine major countries, unlike baseball's so-called "World Series" – which involved, in fact, only two nations,

Canada and the USA. At least Carlton did not, as some Americans do, refer to cricketers as "cricketeers"...

An interesting man, Carlton. He arranges lectures and appearances for clients as disparate as Simon Wiesenthal, the Nazi-hunter from Vienna, and Jose Greco, the Spanish dancer. Once he realised with some alarm that he had booked Greco into a club owned by the Mafia and that Greco, moreover, on seeing the floor, had found it unsuitable – not properly sprung for Spanish dancing. Carlton reported to the Mob that Greco wouldn't dance at their place as the floor was unsuitable, whereupon a large man with a gravelly voice lifted Carlton by the lapels until his weight was off the floor, then said carefully into his face in sepulchral tones:

You tell Greco he dances here tomorrow night, or he don't dance nowhere ever again.

Greco danced. That's how cricket captains with very fast bowlers in their teams operate. When they decide, the opposing batsmen dance. And the morality is exactly the same. Sixty years ago Australia and Britain nearly broke off diplomatic relationships because the England captain, Douglas Jardine, introduced bodyline bowling – directing his fast bowlers to use physical intimidation by aiming directly at the batsmen.

He tried to disguise this Mafia-style tactic with the innocuous name of "fast leg theory", but nothing could obscure the fact that it was a resort to the antithesis of the spirit of cricket. It had been, in fact, dishonourable.

It is hard to explain to American friends the idea of the spirit of a game. They know the phrase "It's not cricket!" and they even use it sometimes, but in the United States the contract is the thing, the stated deal, the terms, the regulations, and they don't see the power of an abstract concept prevailing over the rules. A Los Angeles film maker some years ago couldn't believe that a writer had concluded a film deal with Sir Richard Attenborough on the basis of a handshake rather than a formal contract. The Hollywood man said: "Brother, that wouldn't work in Los Angeles where the saying is – my word is emphatically not my bond!"

He couldn't see that it was the opposite in London, that Attenborough would be far more severely damaged by a whisper at the bar of the Garrick Club that he hadn't kept his word, than by a whole truckload of signed contracts. That is what the culture of honour and the concept "It's not cricket" rests upon, and it is immensely powerful. And it is partly because Jardine forgot, or ignored, or did not understand this spirit of cricket, that there is still so much resentment against the English in Australia.

Whatever other excitements the 1992 World Cup would generate, it seemed certain even weeks before the start of the tournament that the old England-Australia needle would be a feature of it, especially after it was reported that Ian Botham – one of the most gifted Englishmen at needling Australians with bat, ball or words – let it be known that he looked forward to beating the Australian team "before an audience of 100,000 convict-descendants"!

The hype was on...
When it emerged from my conversation with an Indian waiter in New York that I was heading for the World Cup he developed an expression of longing and said: "Ah, just to see the World Cup!"

I said: "I'll think of you as I watch Tendulkar bat ..."

He gave a wail of envy, followed by a soft murmur, as if in prayer: "Ah, to watch Sachin Tendulkar bat! In the World Cup!"

We stood for a moment of cultural closeness among the alien New Yorkers, united as we were in a cricket brotherhood of many nations and ages, and I thought of how often in New York, Chicago and even Los Angeles taxi-drivers from Pakistan, Jamaica, India, Kenya and elsewhere in the former British Empire responded to the opportunity to talk cricket in this mighty nation where, strange thought, many millions knew absolutely nothing about the great game.

As one who has been going on lecture tours of the United States for more than twelve years in all fifty states, I have on many occasions found myself placating the cricketing gods in this cricketingly godless society by enacting a healing ritual in deserted corridors of hotels in cities from Indianapolis to Detroit, from Denver to San Diego, from Laramie to Durango – a series of simulated square-cuts, on-drives, off-breaks and leg-breaks – to bring something of the sanctity and sanity of cricket to the air-space of the deprived. It is a form of exorcism designed to help those unfortunates in thrall to other and lesser sports.

Not that all lesser sports are without merit. Over the years of my lecturing travels in America I developed an interest in baseball, becoming a supporter of the Boston Red Sox in the great years of Jim Rice – very like Viv Richards in his approach to batting. But essentially I found that baseball hadn't the dimensions of interest of cricket. For instance, pitching is entirely aerial, making no use of ground as an extra element; the strike zone, without stumps to hit, is a less spectacular target for the pitcher, and the baseball batter has only one basic stroke, a lateral swing of the bat, and a restricted scoring zone, whereas the cricket batsman has many stroke options – straight drive, off-drive, cover-drive, square cut, late cut, leg glance, hook, pull, on-drive – and can score through a 360-degree arc without any foul line.

Yet baseball is in some ways a more logical game. It has no anomalies like the leg-bye, whose rationale I have never comprehended. Consider the leg-bye. A bowler sends down a good ball which beats the batsman completely, eluding his bat and rapping him on the pad, and for this achievement the bowler's team is penalised one or more runs if the angle at which the ball comes from the pads or body of the beaten batsman – a matter of total luck – in turn eludes the fielders. This nonsense of the leg-bye makes cricket the only sport that imposes a penalty on one sportsman, the bowler, who outperforms another, the beaten batsman.

There's nothing like that in baseball...
Nor, the cricket ball being slightly harder than the baseball, has there ever been any logical reason why some form of fielding glove shouldn't be permitted in cricket, there being no particular merit in professional sportsmen needlessly risking broken fingers and knuckles for considerations unconnected with skill.

Furthermore, cricket has long been the only game in which a draw could be achieved purely by the vagaries of the weather. One team could score a thousand, and its opponents only ten runs for nine wickets, but if rain then washed out play the game was pronounced a draw! And efforts to decide on definite results in rain-affected one-day matches were leading to ever more bizarre procedures.

One suspects that if cricket had grown in popularity in America over the past hundred years certain such "traditions" would long ago have been challenged in the more rational New World. There are few things more worthy of preservation than good traditions, and few things sillier than the preservation of silly traditions merely because they are traditions.

And yet, surprisingly perhaps, the oldest international fixture in the world occurred in North America. As Ralph Dellor reminds us, "in 1844, thirty years before the first Test between Australia and England, Canada played against the United States. In 1859, the first cricket tour in history took place. An English side captained by George Parr of Nottinghamshire met in the George Hotel in Liverpool before setting sail on the 'Nova Scotian' to the United States and Canada. Other tourists followed, In 1882 a third English touring team included W.G. Grace. In 1878 the first Australian team arrived in Canada and included in its ranks many of the players who had appeared in the inaugural Test in Melbourne a year earlier. Cricket was played extensively until the civil war in the 1860's when the troops turned to baseball – perhaps because it was so much easier to throw down four sacks as bases than to find an acceptable cricket pitch. When the soldiers went home, they took baseball with them and it became established at the expense of cricket."

These days when you get to places like Toronto and Philadelphia it is strange to recall that W.G. Grace played cricket in both cities, as in New York, and though the game was more formally structured in the United States in those days, there are today more cricket clubs and more club members playing the game there than ever before.

There are cricket leagues in St. Louis, Los Angeles, San José, San Francisco, Washington, New York, Boston, Philadelphia and many other cities in the U.S., although many of the players are foreigners. Years ago I knew what was called in those days a Rhodesian, who was captain of the Brooklyn Cricket Club, which played in one of three metropolitan cricket leagues in New York City. They played their matches on public parks, usually on matting, and always felt the lack of sight-screens. On the eve of one match on Staten Island my friend and his clubmates laboured long and late to erect two makeshift sight-screen of canvas on bamboo, but when they arrived for the match the following morning both sight-screens were gone.

The groundkeeper said: "Say, I found some kinda sails on boards here this morning – dunno who put 'em up – but I figured they might interfere with your vision so I had 'em taken down."

It is, after all, a massive culture gap...

Yet cricketers persist in the U.S., playing out league fixtures regardless of inferior amenities, and the game survives in some surprising parts of the continent. I once met an entire Mexico City cricket team on a tour of California, and they told me there were fourteen clubs in Mexico.

One afternoon I flipped through the television channels in my Manhattan hotel room to see, to my astonishment, Viv Richards jumping out to loft a four over the bowler's head. Cricket on television in New York! Intrigued, I phoned the TV station to be told it was by popular request, New York apparently having 1.5 million persons originating from cricket-playing countries like Jamaica, Trinidad, Barbados and elsewhere in the Caribbean.

A hundred years or so ago, of course, when W. G. Grace and other stars used to bring touring teams to the U.S., cricket was indigenously American in cities like Philadelphia, and one of the greatest medium-fast swing bowlers in history was Bart King of that city, who was said to have based his exceptional swerve on the curve trajectory he had achieved as a baseball pitcher.

King's nephew, Paul O'Neill of Newport, Rhode Island, was U.S. Consul-General in South Africa in the early seventies, and confirmed some of the legendary accounts about his distinguished uncle, if not the legends themselves. One told of how a touring team had arrived in Philadelphia proclaiming the belief of its three leading batsmen that Bart King was greatly over-rated and would soon be reduced to his proper stature when they batted.

According to the story, when each of these three took his place at the wicket King waved all fielders off the field except deep fine leg, then bowled all three batsmen with identical balls – very late inswingers which clipped the leg bail before running down to the solitary fine-leg fielder. Asked sarcastically why, in view of such accuracy, he needed any fielder at all King replied that he hadn't, but that fine leg was there merely to return the ball to avoid delay ...

However true or untrue the legends, Bart King was undoubtedly a major cricketing personality and had at least one outstanding tour of England during which he became established as the most admired swerve bowler of his time, being bracketed with George Hirst by batsmen who faced both. He was certainly the leading personality of American cricket on the East Coast.

On the West Coast, in Southern California, the undisputed king of cricket was for many years Sir C. Aubrey Smith, the beetle-browed character actor, who as a young cricketer had captained the first representative England side to South Africa. Because of his curved run-up to the wicket when bowling he was nicknamed "Round the Corner" Smith, and one of his best batsmen in the Hollywood Cricket Club was an Englishman whose acting name was Boris Karloff – best known in those days as the Frankenstein Monster. The club still has a fine action picture of him playing an elegant off-drive.

Their friend Hopalong Cassidy asked to play in one of their matches, but wouldn't listen to any advice about keeping a straight bat and kept making baseball-type passes in the air while calling out: "Start pitchin'!"

Among their more successful recruits were Will Rogers, the cowboy philosopher, who might have played before as he had once run a rodeo in Natal, South Africa; David Niven, who had played cricket at school in England, and the South African actor, Basil Rathbone, well known for his portrayals of Sherlock Holmes, who had played the game at school in Johannesburg.

In Los Angeles as I prepared to fly to Sydney for the start of the World Cup I heard about preparations being made in various parts of Southern California for satellite-relayed reports from Australia and New Zealand on the cricket, and it seemed, suddenly, that maybe Los Angeles wasn't quite that remote an outpost of unlikely cricket. Perhaps that award had to go to Moscow, where Mr Harold Wilson was once chased off a cricket pitch by Russian police. Intrigued by this story, I telephoned the former Prime Minister some years ago to check its accuracy and he confirmed that it was indeed true. The incident had occurred when he, as President of the Board of Trade, had led a trade delegation to the Soviet Union and had organised a Sunday cricket match between his delegation and the British Embassy staff.

They had pitched stumps in a public park in central Moscow whereupon the local police, suspicious of anything they didn't understand, had ordered the foreigners to cease the strange ritual immediately. Their commanding officer had actually intruded on to the pitch and gesticulated at the Englishmen. I asked the former Prime Minister how he had got around the situation and he gave a hearty laugh, saying in his Yorkshire accent:

I moved the chap to square leg and we got on with the game. We ignored him and played on, and after a while he left.

Lest thoughts of all connection between cricket and matters Russian might seem too far-fetched, it is well to remember the case of Alexei Bastov, brought as an infant from St. Petersburg by his exiled father in 1918 and placed in an English public school. There he became such a good cricketer that when the Second World War broke out and Alexei, by now in the RAF, was posted to Egypt at the age of 22, he became one of the leading batsmen at the famous Gezira Club where Wally Hammond captained teams containing international cricketers from several countries. He produced so many impressive innings for the club that Hammond enthused over the batting of the young Russian, telling Bill Edrich later that Bastov tended to make his highest scores against the strongest opposition, and certainly looked good enough to be able to play for England after the war.

However, on the morning of an important inter-services match Bastov was missing from his quarters and was never seen again. There were several rumours about his disappearance, one being that he had been spirited away by military intelligence to undertake a top secret mission, and another that he had been murdered by Soviet communists for being related to the Russian aristocracy. Hammond felt at the time that if Bastov had survived the England eleven would have had its first Russian member.

And, while on the subject of cricket exotica, was not one of the leading batsmen playing for Sussex and England around the turn of the century the Nawab of Nawanagar, Kumar Sri Jam Sahib Ranjitsinhji – affectionately known to his English fans as "Smith"?

Ralph Dellor tells a story from Italy which shows how cricket can spread over geographical, political and even religious boundaries, "Some years ago a team from Derbyshire went there on a short tour. When in Rome, an Anglican parson from Belper bowled left arm round the wicket from the Vatican End. Could there possibly be a better illustration of cricket as a world game?"

But enough! Cricket in Los Angeles, cricket by Russians, cricket for England by Indian Maharajahs, cricket in the Vatican – these thoughts and anecdotes were all swirling through my mind as I set off for Los Angeles airport to board my flight to Australia for the World Cup, and while it was legitimate – in fact appropriate – at such a time to remember the depth and sweep of cricket's considerable history, the time had now come to prepare for the latest of the game's great tournaments. Though happy as always to recall pioneers of cricket in distant places and to celebrate the universality of the great game, I now had to narrow such considerations down to focus finally on contention for the 1992 World Cup.

This, then, was what that focus was down to – the last stages of the contest between the countries where the game's flame burned brightest, and as I boarded the aircraft in Los Angeles bound for Sydney the round-robin preliminaries of the World Cup were only two days away, and the long air journey would afford time for a closer study and assessment of the history and possibilities of the teams about to complete.

Cricket on Bathsheba beach in Barbados.

17

PART ONE

The Contenders

At Los Angeles airport it was clear that a dozen or more of my fellow passengers on the Qantas flight bound for Sydney were also heading for the World Cup. Their conversation and their manner gave them away, and one of them, unaware that he was under observation, actually played a discreet little forward defensive shot as he waited in the queue to check in.

Once airborne I immersed myself in Wisden and in the latest material on the tournament and the teams, and by the time we landed at our refuelling-point in Tahiti I had a pretty fair notion of what I thought the major contenders had to offer, and the elements that constituted their challenge.

What each had to offer was compounded not only of the merits of its team but of that country's cricket character and cricket history, cricket teams bearing unmistakeably the stamp of their national culture.

The obvious team to start with in this survey was that of the country which had invented the game in all its complexity of spirit and law.

ENGLAND
Mythologies and Home Truths

It is tough for the English in international matters, because so many 'foreigners' have inferiority complexes about them, so many have historic grievances towards them, and so many simply resent primacy in human endeavour.

Because England, or rather Britain, at one stage or another claimed and exercised ownership of much of the world, and in its spare time invented or developed many of the leading sports such as cricket, rugby, soccer, tennis, golf, boxing, squash, handball, fives, and other lesser-known activities probably including tiddlywinks, it is a keen priority of certain former colonies to defeat the mother country comprehensively in the sport for which England is most renowned and with which it is most identified – cricket.

And, despite their apparent masochism, and their long history of fortitude in adversity, the English do not take entirely kindly to defeat at the hands of the colonies or ex-colonies. Neville Oliver tells the story of the Oval Test of 1882 against the Australian colonials:

> *It had always been considered that the earlier Colonial victories over England had come about because the best English players had been unavailable. There was a certain amount of home confidence as the teams took the field – a confidence that seemed to be justified as the Australians, batting first, were dismissed for 63. "Demon" Spofforth kept Australia in the match with seven for forty-six as England replied with 101. Australia then made 122, setting England 85 to win, At two for fifty-one things looked simple but that equation did not bargain on Spofforth who took seven for forty-four. England had lost AT HOME by seven runs.*
>
> *One spectator died. It was reported that another gnawed the handle off his umbrella and the scorer was so nervous that he was unable to make legible scratches in the score book.*

Vijay Rana tells of another "golden moment", this time for Sri Lankan cricket, which occurred in August 1984 — "and that, too, at the Mecca of Cricket, Lords. English cricket was being tormented by decaying form and bad luck. The West Indians had just beaten them 5–0. Botham had been tamed, and the captain David Gower was dubbed the protagonist of 'the abstentionist school of captaincy'. The Lord's Test began with hopes of England salvaging some of its lost reputation, but what followed was a great disaster." This provoked – obviously with benefit of hindsight – an anguished leader in *The Guardian*:

> *There were some who said that the five-nil defeats in the Test series against the West Indies marked a new low in the fortunes of English cricket, but we declined to join that chorus out of a proper apprehension about what might follow. The Test match with Sri Lanka, however, can now confidently be entered by all nadir lovers in their record books. England may do as badly in future, but they will not do worse."*

WG Grace: truth.

The author of England's misfortune was Sidath Wettimuny, the first ever Sri Lankan to hit 100 in an official Test, an 157 at Faisalabad in Pakistan in 1982. At Lords he destroyed a pale English attack in a mammoth innings of 190, lasting for over ten hours. "The precise moment at which the nadir was reached," continued the Guardian leader, came when Botham "was hooked three times into the Mound Stand by the excellent Sri Lankan captain Mendis, on Friday afternoon." Mendis reached his hurricane century in just 144 minutes.

There are still some people, observes Mihir Bose, "who believe Neville Cardus' assertion that if everything else about England were lost – her civilisation, her constitution, the Laws of England – cricket would be sufficient to construct an Eternal Englishness."

"There is," says Brian Johnston, "something about cricket which always reminds me of England. That may appear corny, but to me, and thousands like me, that is the way I see the game. Whenever I travel round the country, and pass where a game is being played, I always try to stop for a while to capture that unique atmosphere. Schools, villages and clubs all play throughout the summer and it gives me great pleasure to see the game being played and the players enjoying themselves. Cricket, after all, started with boys and young men hitting a stone with a stick or plank of wood during a break from looking after the animals in the fields, or working in the woods. Many of the terms in the game belong to the countryside. 'Stump' simply refers to a tree stump and the term 'wicket' is more than likely derived from the wicket of the gate of a sheep pen, which the bowler would have aimed at. The bail would have been the cross piece of the gate. The length of the pitch, twenty-two yards, would have been determined by the old country measurement, called a chain."

Yet there is much that is misleading in this popular picture of English cricket full of bucolic charm. As Brian Johnston observes, the international game "in England, as in other parts of the world, had become so serious at the top professional level, that I often find club and village cricket more enjoyable. It is still a great honour to play for England, but I regret that many first-class and international players do not appear to enjoy the game as much as they once did. How often do you see a player *smile* on the pitch?" Portrayed as a gentle pastime, cricket is, on occasion, one of the most dangerous sports known to the human race.

"The whole history of cricket," Johnston comments, "is the endless struggle between bat and ball. The development of the roundarm delivery was one of the most significant steps in the history of the game. The reputed pioneer of this was John Wiles of Kent. He is said to have copied the methods of his sister, who, when bowling to him in practice in the family garden, had to raise her arm level because of her dress. For a while the new bowling method was seen by some as destroying the game. Apart from

W G Grace: Old man of myth.

the new bowling techniques, early batsmen had to contend with dubious pitches. The surfaces were so rough that facing even underarm bowling was a hazardous business. And of course, some underarm bowling was pretty ferocious."

The projection at a player of a hard object at close to a hundred miles an hour – aimed to kick up from the ground at the head, shoulders or torso of a batsman, and more than occasionally hitting some part of him – would be regarded in most sporting codes as beyond the acceptable limit. Let the devotees of such gentler codes be aware that in international cricket this is part of the *accepted* aim and method of fast bowlers during the first hour of play when the ball is new – and sometimes even beyond that stage.

So the image of cricket as the unfailingly calm pursuit of amiable eccentrics, dressed in white, playing for the sheer joy of the game, is somewhat wide of the mark. As Brian Johnston remarks, the motive for many a cricket match is, at least in part, pecuniary. "Many nowadays frown with disapproval at the introduction of sponsors who aim to publicize their company's name in return for financing the game. But that is nothing new. The English country gentry, once they had discovered what their workers were playing, soon began to take an interest, and many of them saw the game as a way of making *money* – not, at the first, by playing themselves, but by organising matches against teams raised by neighbouring gentry and betting huge sums on the result."

Misleading, too, is the usual portrayal of the character who did most to shape modern English cricket. He was, in fact, a tall, slim young athlete who had achieved some renown as a hurdler and sprinter, who on one occasion preceded an innings at Lord's with a morning hurdling race at Wembley, and became known as the most remarkable batsman in the world, transforming the art of batting into a multi-faceted, multi-stroke skill.

But was this handsome young giant the image of the embodiment of English cricket? No, no, no – that would have been far too straightforward. That image was, rather, transformed into that of a fat old autocrat with huge bearded visage beneath a comically tiny cricket cap.

Both had the same name, William Gilbert Grace. In fact, they were the same person, but for purposes of benign legend the image chosen for projection was the man in his old age, rather than the man in his prime.

One of the consequences of such image-substitution was that it became hard to credit the remarkable achievements of the subject. Seeing W.G. Grace as the middle-aged or elderly player, corpulent and grey-bearded, one couldn't envisage the extraordinary feats he performed with bat and ball, nor realise sufficiently that, so great was this man's adaptability to environment and conditions, he would have dominated the game in any era.

There is something in the English character that smacks of reluctance to idolise prominent persons unless they have been made over into another image – in this case Grace's less glamorous, more geriatric image of a kind of father of the nation.

The West Indian-born cricket-writer and polemicist, C.L.R. James, carried out an interesting exercise in imagination to illustrate the greatness of Grace. He translated the exceptional innings and analyses of a hundred years ago to the modern age, quantifying how many runs, how often, the modern batsman would have had to score on bad pitches to build up a comparable record to that of Grace.

Certainly Ian Terence Botham would probably have to pass the age of fifty, become massively corpulent, and ideally qualify as a medical doctor in order to receive his just due at the hands of his compatriots. Although all the evidence indicates that Botham is possibly the greatest figure in English cricket since W.G. Grace, certainly in terms of drawing crowds, and probably the greatest all-rounder in the history of the game, it is highly unlikely that his contemporaries will accord him that reputation until his powerful but rough-and-ready personality has been somewhat forgotten with the passage of the years.

His nearest rival as a great all-rounder, Sir Garfield Sobers, was undoubtedly a greater cricketer than Botham – but not, the facts suggest, a greater all-rounder.

Sobers was certainly a greater batsman, and his all-round gifts were quite extraordinary because he could bowl left arm fast, medium seam, slow left arm regular or back-of-the-hand. But as a bowler he was not the strike force in Test cricket that Botham became. For example, in the same number of Tests Botham took over 370 wickets, compared to Sobers' 235. And he, too, took these wickets with three different types of bowling. Up to the early eighties Botham was a classical medium to medium-fast bowler with a

deadly late outswing and inswing, of the type made famous in England at various times by George Hirst, Maurice Tate and Alec Bedser. Then for a brief period to the middle eighties he became a fast bowler heavily dependant on his ability to make the ball rise, and finally, in the nineties, he became a medium-slow bowler of outstanding accuracy, able not only to swing the ball either way but to cut it sharply off the seam as well.

In the realm of batting Botham, with over 5000 Test runs, is nowhere near the remarkable Sobers total of over 8000 but he is ahead of the catching list, with 115 as against 109 for Sobers. In defining an all-rounder as a cricketer who would be chosen for a team either purely as a bowler or purely as a batsman, and keeping in mind the balance between batting and bowling skills, my submission is therefore that one has to rank Botham ahead of Sobers – a point underlined by the fact that Botham took only 21

Ian Botham Bowling for Somerset against the Australians at Bath in 1977. Dickie Bird is the Umpire, loooking at the batsman as if he hadn't got a chance.

22

Tests to reach the double of 1000 runs and 100 wickets, whereas Sobers took 48 Tests.

Apart from Sobers, then, ranged behind Botham with the latter's 5192 runs, 383 wickets and 118 catches, come the likes of India's Kapil Dev, who on the eve of the World Cup passed Sir Richard Hadlee's total of 431 wickets and also had over 4500 runs, being second only to Botham in the number of Tests taken to achieve the double – 25.

Behind Kapil Dev is an impressive list of great all-rounders, completing the table as follows:

Ian Botham (E) 5192 runs, 383 wickets, in 100 Tests
Gary Sobers (WI) 8032 runs, 235 wickets, in 93 Tests
Kapil Dev (I) 4521 runs, 432 wickets, in 109 Tests
Richie Benaud (A) 2201 runs, 248 wickets, in 63 Tests
Keith Miller (A) 2958 runs, 170 wickets, in 55 Tests
Wilfred Rhodes (E) 2325 runs, 127 wickets, in 58 Tests
Richard Hadlee (NZ) 3124 runs, 431 wickets, in 86 Tests
Imran Khan (P) 3541 runs, 358 wickets, in 82 Tests
Tony Greig (E) 3599 runs, 141 wickets, in 58 Tests
Trevor Bailey (E) 2290 runs, 132 wickets, in 61 Tests
Vinoo Mankad (I) 2109 runs, 162 wickets, in 44 Tests
Ravi Shastri (I) 3372 runs, 143 wickets, in 72 Tests
Trevor Goddard (SA) 2516 runs, 123 wickets, in 41 Tests

One of the considerations making England favourites to win the 1992 World Cup in my opinion was the inclusion of Ian Botham in the England squad. To his value as a hard-hitting batsman could be added his newfound economy of bowling as a one-day player – in marked contrast to his former profligacy when bowling in five-day Tests in search of quick wickets and in readiness to buy them with runs – and his genius as a close slip-field. Indeed, of all the World Cup players included in this tournament, Botham was the only one who would at least have had to come into serious consideration in selection of an all-time great World Eleven.

As a believer in this method of measuring players against each other, I decided early to measure the 1992 World Cup players against their national all-time XIs, selected as if all were in their prime.

I began this exercise as the plane took off from Tahiti for Sydney on the last leg of the flight to the World Cup, and the great advantage of the system was that it was purely arbitrary, being my opinion only, and for purposes of talent-estimation the self-appointed judge's decision (mine) was final, irrevocable and unchallengeable— at least until the next argument with a fellow cricket fanatic ...

Here, then, was my All-Time England XI, listing the

Graham Gooch

Highest Test score of each batsman as a matter of interest:

Hobbs	211
Hutton	364
Rhodes	179
Hammond	336
Grace	170
Compton	278
Botham	208
Ames	149
Larwood	98
Laker	63
Barnes	38
TOTAL	2094

Bowling: Larwood, Barnes, Botham, Hammond, Rhodes, Laker and Grace.
Omitted with regrets: Woolley, May, Sutcliffe, Trueman.

So Ian Botham was the only name common to the above XI and the England squad for the 1992 World Cup. It seemed to me that the best batting line-up for England was:

Gooch
Botham
Stewart
Hick
Smith
Lamb
Fairbrother
Lewis
Ramprakash
De Freitas
Pringle

Bowling: Pringle, Botham, Lewis, Hick, De Freitas.

This team, in my view, put into the field strong batting down to number eleven, with the option of using Gooch as an alternate bowler with Hick or, in the absence of form by the latter, Dermot Reeve as the fifth bowler. It also included the fine fielding of Mark Ramprakash, fielding being one of the keys of the one-day game. The team was also predicated on all-out assault from the first over, with Botham and Gooch ready to hit over the restricted field in the early overs, and a refusal to panic over loss of wickets in view of the long batting line-up. Gooch, however, with a strong streak of caution in his make-up, was more likely to want Gladstone Small or another bowler, requiring something like seven bowlers to permutate, though I liked the notion of the endless batting list.

Again and again it seemed to me, flying that last leg of the journey from Tahiti to Sydney, that England with this line-up would be the hardest team in the whole tournament to beat.

AUSTRALIA

Convicts and Colonists

I was expecting Australia to reach the semi-final at least, not because it was as strong as Australian national teams usually are, but because the Australians would be playing on their home grounds, with their usual spirit, and with public support at all venues.

"Cricket", Neville Oliver reminds us, "is one of the few games played in Australia that captures the interest of the whole nation. During the winter months the country fragments into many interest-groups to follow a vast variety of football codes but in the summer there is only one game for a sports-mad public to follow."

Cricket has, therefore, always had a very special place in the minds of Australians. Before Australia became a united nation, Neville Oliver points out, "the colonies had their first taste of antipodean togetherness with cricket victories. The passionate loyalty to the individual States which still affects Test selection is a reminder of the difficulty of binding the colonies together into a country. In times of crisis, such as the Great Depression of the nineteen-thirties, cricket gave Australians a chance to focus on things other than the severe times in which they were living."

As is the case with so many countries, cricket has both healed and exacerbated the tensions which exist between the different communities that make up the 'nation'. On many of their early tours, Neville Oliver tells us, the Australian players "kept to their own colonial groupings. Arguments and inter-colonial rivalries were forever present, On the 1886 tours the settlement of internal bickering turned into almost a full-time job for the captain, Henry Scott. Later Spofforth would say:

The rivalry is not limited to the field. It extends from society to politics, to every side of life.

The tour was a disaster, on and off the field. Australia lost the Test series three-one."

Cricket in Australia has been free of the class divisions, the distinctions between "gentlemen" and "players'" that was such a mark of the English game. Australians never adopted the "apartheid" of amateurs and professionals. On the other hand, divisions which are less marked in England (though strongly marked in Britain), have had serious effects on Australian cricket. Along with the interstate rivalries, at least one touring side was fundamentally split by religion. According to Neville Oliver, Bradman "grew up in a country where religious bigotry was a fact of life. Job advertisements of the nineteen-thirties proudly bannered: 'Catholics need not apply'. That mentality spilled into all walks of life including Australian cricket."

Racialism, proper, has not caused Australian cricket much trouble – largely because so few aborigines seem to be interested in the game. Not many have reached first class standards and those that have did not have happy careers. In the 1880s the fast bowler, Jack March, was accused of throwing. Another bowler, Eddie Gilbert, came from an aboriginal settlement near Brisbane. He did not take kindly to wearing boots. His action, too, was suspected. He was accused of employing techniques developed while throwing his boomerang. He turned to drink and, at the age of forty, having lost the power of speech, was taken into care.

Nevertheless, the Australian national side is always bound together, with a unity that is the envy of other nations, under one particular stimulus – the chance of beating England. In this World Cup the matches between Australia and England were expected to be particularly well-fought. Where both these countries and their teams are at their best, contests between them remain the pinnacle of international cricket. When Australia first beat England, in a Test Match in 1887, there began the process whereby England, who invented cricket and taught it to her fledgling colonies, began to have it taught back to them by these same developing offspring.

Defeat at the hands of Australia is often resented by Englishmen – a resentment the Australians are quick to return. Among some Australians the bitterness stems from the fact that Australia was used as a convict settlement (even though most of the "convicts" hadn't been criminals in the commonly accepted sense of the word, and many of them had been highly impressive persons – political leaders campaigning for Irish independence or for other unpopular causes of the time).

During the visit of an English team led by Lord Harris in 1878-9 a Sydney mob – equally upset by an umpiring decision and a remark from one of the English professionals concerning the origins of their opponents – stormed onto the pitch endangering the players. Neville Oliver tells the story:

> *Lord Harris travelled with his own umpire – an Australian named George Coulthard. Coulthard gave the popular Billy Murdoch out to a dubious decision in the New South Wales second innings. Stirred up by bookmakers, a mob invaded the ground. Lord Harris refused to continue the match but remained on the ground until he was struck with a stick and play was abandoned for the day. The next morning a local paper carried a story that two English players had called sections of the crowd 'nothing but the sons of convicts' – a gibe which at that time, and until fairly recently, was probably the most derogatory remark that could be made to a colonial.*

In more recent times English players have been known to raise their arms to the Australian crowds, wrists together as if manacled.

This British attitude goes a long way towards explaining the hurt and incomprehension that was widely felt in Australia during Douglas Jardine's "bodyline" series. Although Neville Oliver says wryly:

> *The only remaining mystery about the much-discussed series is the failure of the Australians on this occasion to fight fire with fire. It is not in the cricketing make-up of the Australian Test player to turn the other cheek. But under a captain who actually believed in the spirit of the game every rule can have its exceptions.*

It is partly because of Jardine's tactics that there is still so much ill-feeling in Australia towards the "Pommies". The Australians, after all, had been taught their cricket by the English, and though they played it hard, some really did believe in the spirit of the game (as indeed did some in England). Australian cricket and Australian society developed side by side under the uncertain direction of the first English military settlers. The first Australian players learned their cricket from touring English professionals and English coaches. The first touring English sides (one was led by W.G. Grace himself) had been

Cheerfully insulting banners on the first day of the Fourth Test between Australia and England at Melbourne in December 1982.

generally treated with courtesy and respect. Later relations during Australian tours of England were less amicable. The Australian team, as Neville Oliver says "showed massive irritation when the umpire's decisions went against them. Over another incident W.G. Grace called them 'a nasty lot of sneaks'." But these disputes were as nothing to the row over the bowling of Jardine's team. For when the Australians saw a captain of England discard the fundamental spirit of cricket simply in order to win, and in discarding it show a readiness to inflict serious physical injury on opponents, it created a deep and lasting disillusionment with the sense of values of the mother country which overlay already complex attitudes and emotions springing from the historical relationship between the two countries.

Some of the first signs of the fighting spirit of Australian cricket had been given by the 'Demon', F. R. Spofforth, in 1878. Australia were playing MCC at Lords. Spofforth overheard the disparaging comments of one more-than-usually- pompous member who expressed surprise that the visiting Australians were not black – "like the last lot" (a reference to the first team to visit England from Australia which had been drawn entirely from the aborigines). Spofforth's reply was terrible but entirely within the spirit of cricket. He took ten MCC wickets for twenty in that match, and went on to destroy English batsmen throughout the 1880s. However, it is also entirely according to the spirit of cricket that, just as Jardine's weapon (or victim), Larwood, ended his days in Australia, so Spofforth spent his declining years as a much-loved English resident.

Clouding this coming World Cup was also the belief which seems to be growing among many Australians that Britain had callously and needlessly sent many Australians to their deaths at Gallipoli in the First World War, and had been prepared to "write off" Australia to the Japanese in World War Two. Such resentments, whether justified or not, were an overlay on a basic feeling among many Australians that the English looked down on many of them as crude colonials – a belief backed up partially by the fact that this has indeed been a view of Australians held in certain quarters in England.

These various prejudices, held in varying degrees of seriousness on both sides, have certainly made for lively cricket contests between England and Australia, and, for that matter, lively contests in a whole range of sports.

On the healthiest level it is a family dispute featuring mutual jibing and a rivalry based on the closeness of two countries in basic matters of culture, language, and political values. On the unhealthiest level it is a snide inter-sniping based more on ignorance than on knowledge of each others' essential qualities. Sometimes, regrettably, cricket contests between Australia and England produce a particular bitterness and small-mindedness.

However, the bowling strength of the Australian national team for the 1992 World Cup was, I felt, overrated, and unlikely to muster the necessary aggression. An initial mistake made by the Australian selectors had surely been the omission of Simon O'Donnell, one of the best one-day all-rounders in the world.

He had, said the selectors, been off form. When will selectors learn to pick for class and not form? Form is something that can return in seconds; class cannot be acquired in a lifetime. The South African selectors once dropped the brilliant Roy McLean (for attacking the bowling "too recklessly") in favour of a steady, orthodox batsman called Derek Varnals, who was said to be "in form". The result was national frustration as South Africans saw a Test Match slip through their fingers because Varnals couldn't get the ball past the fielders – and could hardly get it off the square. A match that should have been won with several overs to spare was drawn. A class player even out of form would have finished the job or got out quickly so that someone else could.

Still, even without O'Donnell, the Australian batting looked strong, though it contained no players who would have gained a place in my all-time Australian eleven:

Highest Score

Ponsford	266
Trumper	214
Bradman	334
G. Chappell	247
Harvey	205
Miller	147
Marsh	132
Lindwall	118
Lillee	73
O'Reilly	56
Iverson	1
TOTAL	793

Bowling: Lillee, Lindwall, Miller, Iverson, O'Reilly.
Omitted with regret: Border, Macartney, McCabe, J.Gregory

The closest of the current World Cup squad to this list was obviously Allan Border, one of the greatest players in Australian cricket history, who had already played in more Tests and scored more runs than any other Australian, although the following little statistic provides a telling measure between the great Don Bradman and the merely human Allan Border:

> Border 8701 runs, 23 centuries, in 115 Tests
> Bradman 6996 runs, 29 centuries, in 52 Tests

Here, on the eve of their first match of the 1992 World Cup, was the probable Australian line-up:

> Moody
> Taylor
> Boon
> Jones
> S.Waugh
> M.Waugh
> Border
> Healy
> McDermott
> Reid
> Whitney

> Bowling: McDermott, Reid, Whitney, Waugh, Moody.

Allan Border

The bowling looked a bit thin to me. Whitney, though accurate and steady, had never seemed to have the class of an international bowler, and Reid, very impressive in Test Matches, still carried the stigma of yielding 18 runs off a final over to give England a win in a one-day game. Moody, too, was very much a part-time bowler, and McDermott and Steve Waugh looked to be the best of a fairly second-rate attack. Thus while I expected Australia to reach the semi-final, I didn't expect them to reach the final.

So far, then, my predicted semi-finalists were England, and Australia. The third and fourth were still to be selected.

INDIA
Hotheads and Princes

The consummate artists of world cricket in style, elegance and beauty of stroke-play seem to be produced more often in India than in any other country – though to speak of that enormous place as a 'country' seems inappropriate. It is a sub-continent.

But country or continent, when I have visited India I have not felt I was in a foreign land, largely because of the many English-language newspapers and publications and shared political and cultural values – including cricket and the ready availability in India of cricket scores of significance from all over the world. India is a place where things cricketing touch the heart.

According to Vijay Rana, "cricket is one of the few positive legacies of the British

Empire. The greatest paradox in Indian cricket is Calcutta. Since the seventies the state of West Bengal has been ruled by the marxist CPIM party, which has co–existed reasonably happily with India's largest capitalist enterprises in the region. Yet Calcutta has provided passionate Indian cricket crowds. The city has seen Test riots, it has booed the legendary Sunil Gavaskar for slow scoring, and has seen a World Cup cricket final. It is a wry Indian saying that by the twenty-first century, the only true communists and true Englishmen will be found in India."

"Indian cricket," comments Mihir Bose, "unlike West Indian cricket, has never been a cement for nationalism – for the simple reason that there are more potent symbols available."

Throughout South Asia cricket has survived through historical bonds and political continuity. In this part of the empire, including Sri Lanka, comments Vijay Rana "political independence came through well structured nationalist movements, rather than by violent revolution. Many political leaders were educated in English schools, where they learned to play cricket. The bureaucracy was largely controlled by the Indian native elite, which had flourished under their colonial masters. Such was the class that the famous historian Thomas Babbington Macaulay, a member of the Indian governor

Cricket among the Sacred Cows and townspeople of Bombay.

general's Supreme Council, had intended to create. In 1835, when he was laying the foundations of English education in India he envisaged a class of native collaborators, or, as he put it: 'A class of persons ... English in taste, in opinions, in morals and in intellect.' During the Raj, playing cricket with the English brought these Indians all the social advantages of moving in colonial high society. After Independence, it was this class, powerful in government and influential in society, which patronized cricket. Their sons didn't go to Oxford or Cambridge but to elite schools in Sri Lanka, where the cricket tradition was enthusiastically kept up."

In this way, as in many others, Indian cricket has, according to Mihir Bose "more than the cricket of other countries, reflected India's history. If everything about India were to be destroyed, a history of Indian cricket would serve as an outline of the history of the nation and give important clues to national character. Indians are probably the world's greatest optimists. They are always ready to believe that round the next corner will emerge a leader who will solve everything, that the next series will miraculously conjure up a world-beating cricket team. Some of this is due to the Indian belief in the circular theory of time where a dark age is supposed to be replaced by a glorious one before it is in turn destroyed by another dark age. Such a view of the world contributes to the extraordinary faith, in the redemptive power of the leader. The majority of Indians are not Christians and do not share the vision of a Christian Messiah, but they do believe in a leader who can set the world to rights. And often enough in Indian history a leader has arrived, quite unexpectedly, and has taken on the world and emerged triumphant. It is this that prevents Indians from reading their history and going mad. They need faith if only not to believe that the future cannot be as awful as the past."

India is, in fact, one of the first cricketing countries after England. The first recorded cricket was played in 1721 in Cambay in the west, though the game developed more quickly in the eastern part of the country – specifically Calcutta where the famous Calcutta Cricket Club was formed in 1792. Five years later the first formal match in Bombay was arranged, and thereafter cricket progressed apace in various parts of India.

"Cricket," as Mihir Bose tells the story, "was introduced to India by expatriate British sailors on a beach in western India. It grew not because the British encouraged it but because individual Indians took it up. First the Parsees in Bombay, making that the centre of Indian cricket, followed by the Indian Princes. It is now fashionable to decry the princes but, while Indian cricket might have developed without the Princes, it would not have developed so quickly or with such a flourish. The Princes brought an exotic royal style that was quite unique. The most colourful was undoubtedly Bhupendra Singh of Patiala. On the field he introduced the princely slog, once making 86 exclusively in fours and sixes. Off the field his womanising became a legend. One critic wrote that while the Englishman started the day with bacon and eggs and the Frenchman with rolls, the Maharajah started with a virgin. In the grounds of his palace, which also housed three hundred women and concubines and a scented swimming pool, was a lovely cricket ground where he brought some of the best professionals of the day: Hirst, Rhodes, Leyland, Larwood, Waddington, Kilner, and the Australians, Frank Tarrant, Bromley and Scaife."

The first Indian tour to England was in 1886, but it was only after Indian Independence that Indian teams began to challenge England realistically in terms of equal skill and confidence. The Princes had become an impediment to cricketing success. "For almost two decades in the thirties and forties," says Mihir Bose, "when India was finding her feet in international cricket, the overriding question was not to build a team but to find a Prince – any Prince – to captain the side. The Maharajah of Porbander captained the team touring England in 1932. He played in the first four matches scoring 0, 2, 0, 2, 2, and ending with a 'first-class' average of 0.66. He was said to be the only first-class cricketer to have more Rolls Royces than runs. So while the Princes may have made cricket fashionable they also introduced the worm of jealousy and intrigue that remains the bane of Indian cricket – perhaps Indian life. If Bombay is as strong as it normally is, having won the Ranji trophy 31 times since its start in 1934, then Delhi, Calcutta and Madras are constantly plotting its downfall. For this reason India, despite the astonishing array of individual talent, seldom blended into a team."

And yet today India is one of the most highly regarded cricketing powers, being a former winner of the World Cup and possessing (with Australia) the most capacious cricket stadiums in the world.

The greatest change that has occurred in Indian cricket in recent years is that since that World Cup triumph of 1983 the country which used to be more dedicated to Test Cricket than any other has forsaken that form of the for the one-day game. This came as no surprise to Mihir Bose:

I grew up in India during the years when cricket rose in popularity through the nineteen fifties and sixties, the increasing urbanisation bringing an ever-growing mass of population to the cities hungry for this new fiesta, wonder, excitement. This finally culminated in the much heralded Test fever – when a city where a Test was being played seemed to be in the grip of a certain kind of madness, thinking of nothing but cricket and with every individual, it seemed, in search of a ticket to see the match. Life only returned to normal when the match was over and the circus left town.

The visitor arriving in the city could readily misunderstand this fervour as deep-rooted enthusiasm for Test cricket, but, while there was a genuine love and understanding of the game the

Cricket matches being played in the public area of the Azad Maided in Bombay.

fever was produced by the Indian craving for "tamasha", for fiesta, spectacle. The spectacle happened to be a Test Match. It might have been a parade of film stars, as it so often is, or the circus. But even at the height of Test cricket fever, it was noticeable that such enthusiasm did not extend to domestic cricket which was, and continues to be, poorly supported.

Once India had won the World Cup, allegiance switched. Test cricket lost its ability to generate mass hysteria: one-day cricket instantly took over. No revolution could have been more quickly accomplished or more complete. One-day cricket with its instant excitement and instant results fits the Indian mood more easily. The outsider visiting India and arriving with the mental baggage of images of a slow ancient people toiling patiently in a hot land may find this hard to believe. But while these images are not necessarily wrong — it is an ancient land: it is hot: people do toil slowly: there is an Indian trick here. Indians themselves are the world's most impatient people. The favourite Indian expression is the word juldi, hurry. It is common in Indian restaurants and offices to feel that a mini-earthquake is taking place: tables at which you are seated seem to be gently rocking. But it is not an earthquake. It is only the Indians tapping their feet. Some have suggested that this endless tapping of the feet is a sign of a search for inner harmony. I see it as an indication of an inner impatience. It is this impatience, this desire for instant gratification that one-day cricket satisfies and satisfies very well.

My all-time Indian team is particularly strong with batting of the highest rank down to number eight, and a good balanced bowling attack. Omitted with regret were the likes of Merchant, Viswanath, Nayudu, Amar Singh and Azharuddin.

Here is the team with the highest Test scores:

Gavaskar	236
Shastri	187
Vinoo Mankad	231
Ranjitsinhji	175
Tendulkar	148
Pataudi	203
Kapil Dev	163
Engineer	121
Bedi	50
Prasanna	37
Nissar	4
TOTAL	1565

Bowling: Kapil Dev, Nissar, Tendulkar, Bedi, Prasanna, Mankad and Shastri.
Omitted with regret: Duleepsinhji, Azharuddin, Viswanath.

India's squad for the World Cup was, on paper, one of the strongest in the tournament — but an unusually arduous touring schedule shortly before the World Cup diminished their chances, in my view, of winning the trophy again this time. Still, their probable first-choice batting line-up was impressive enough:

Krish Srikkanth
Ravi Shastri
Dilip Vengsarkar

Sanjay Manjrekar
Sachin Tendulkar
Mohammad Azharuddin
Kapil Dev
Kiran More
Manoj Prabhakar
Subroto Banerjee
Anil Kumble

Bowling: Banerjee, Dev, Prabhakar, Shastri, Kumble.

So Tendulkar, Shastri and Kapil Dev were the names common to both lists. Obviously if the Indians could overcome the injuries and strains consequent on their tough pre-tournament tour in Australia, they could be a formidable force with the brilliant Tendulkar to the fore.

It was being said, furthermore, that young Tendulkar was now blossoming as a tight medium-pace bowler ideally suited to the one-day game. India might be even more of a threat than I had supposed as I continued my pre-tournament analysis of various national and team strengths.

NEW ZEALAND

Lambs to the Slaughter?

As New Zealand had only one great player in Martin Crowe, no bowlers of exceptional ability, and only one other batsman who might conceivably dominate an attack – Mark Greatbatch – I couldn't see them as a major factor in the tournament. Greatbatch was completely out of form and England had just completed a one-sided series of Test matches as well as one-day matches against New Zealand in New Zealand in which the home team had been comprehensively beaten.

New Zealand cricket had made enormous strides over the past three decades and had even, in the late eighties, reached the top rank of Test-playing countries. But since the retirement of the great Richard Hadlee the team had, in my opinion, declined considerably in class.

Cricket in New Zealand, as Iain Gallaway points out, was dominated in its early years "by the leading figures in the communities, business, pastoral and professional who certainly controlled its administration, and probably the playing." In the summer of 1851 the Christchurch.Cricket Club advertised its office bearers and its first practice date:

> *Gentlemen desirous of becoming members are requested to communicate with the Hon. Secretaries. Annual sub 10/6. Entrance fee 10/6.*

"The invitation," says Iain Gallaway, "to gentlemen seems to have been accepted literally. The team which played in the first recorded match on 16th December 1851 reads like a Who's Who of Christchurch society. Strangely enough their opponents were the Working Man's Club."

When the City of Dunedin held a cricket carnival attended by a team from England which included W.G. Grace, the visitors, as Iain Gallaway tells us, travelled to Dunedin by the following procession:

> *Two mounted troopers*
> *Party of horsemen from Port Chalmers*
> *Port Chalmers Club*
> *All England XI in a coach with six white horses driven by*
> *"Cabbage Tree Ned"*
> *Mr Shadrach Jone's private carriage*
> (Mr Shadrach Jones was the promoter of the tour.)
> *Match Committee and the Dunedin Club*
> *North Dunedin Club Tokomario Club*
> *Two coaches of cricketers*
> *Citizens in private vehicles, well decorated*
> *Horsemen three abreast*

Despite such local pageantry, for many years New Zealand cricket was been treated as a sort of poorer cousin of the Australians, of England – of everybody. The champion New Zealand team had ventured to Australia in the late eighteen-seventies with, as Iain Gallaway puts it, "satisfactory playing but disastrous financial results. New Zealand's first official overseas tour to Australia was in 1898-9. The national team was poorly chosen and suffered overwhelming defeats at the hands of the two first-class states – Victoria and New South Wales. Fifteen years later a visiting team did better that their predecessors but still lost by an innings to both these states."

In the old days teams would only tour New Zealand if such tours were tacked on, like afterthoughts, to tours of Australia. Obviously distance was a factor in the days when cricket teams travelled only by sea. "After the nineteen-twenties," says Iain Gallaway, "visits from Australian teams became less frequent. From 1927 to 1928 not a single team visited New Zealand. A gap of over forty years separates New Zealand's first Test against England and the second official Test between the near neighbours. It is not surprising that, whilst victory over Australia in any sport is sweet to a New Zealander, victory in cricket is something to be relished, savoured, dwelt on."

Iain Gallaway describes the state of New Zealand cricket after the Second World War:

> We were, whether we liked it on not, the poor relations, the amateurs against the professionals, boys against men. While some of our performances, both individually and collectively, were, from time to time, quite sensationally good, there was a lack of consistency which cost our international reputation dearly. We were still club cricketers, Saturday afternooners. Never was that more starkly illustrated than in the first 'Test' I ever saw at my home ground, Carisbrook, in January 1936. I watched fascinated as the combined might of New Zealand accumulated 81 runs in answer to a little matter of 853 for 5 declared from a MCC team which contained only three players with Test experience.

New Zealand occasionally produced one or two great players, but never a great team of players, and these were generally batsmen, so that even if New Zealand teams scored well against other countries they were seldom able to bowl them out. They had, however, a great reputation for determination in the face of adversity. Dick Brittenden once gave a remarkable account of a remarkable match on the South African tour of 1952-3 when, at Ellis Park in Johannesburg, New Zealand wrote one of the most stirring passages not just in their own but in the entire history of cricket.

> On the morning of the second day, word was received that the fiancée of Bob Blair, the side's fast bowler, had lost her life in a train disaster which claimed one hundred and fifty people. Blair stayed in his hotel room when the players went to the ground.
>
> After taking the last two South African wickets, the New Zealanders went in to face a very young and very vigorous Neil Adcock. They were regularly struck by the ball rearing from a lively, even dangerous pitch. Two retired hurt. Lawrie Miller departed, coughing blood. Sutcliffe sustained a fearful blow behind an ear. At hospital he fainted twice. John Reid took five sickening blows in his twenty-five minutes of batting.
>
> Soon after lunch, New Zealand's score stood at 59 for five, with two batsmen hors de combat. Unexpectedly Miller came in again. He left at 82 for six. Then Sutcliffe emerged into the white light, his head turbanned in bandages, his face pale as parchment. All brilliance and bravery, he attacked, hitting seven sixes in an innings of 80 not out. But the most poignant moment came

with the fall of the ninth wicket, The players began to leave the field, Sutcliffe included They stopped; and the silence was immense when Blair emerged from the gloom of the tunnel. Sutcliffe went to meet him, put a compassionate arm about his shoulder. Then, the most touching, unforgettable gesture: Blair brushing his glove across his eyes before taking the first ball. The pair batted together for ten minutes. They scored 33, Blair adding a six to Sutcliffe's soaring, graceful strokes.

Clearly character and courage were factors to be taken into account when considering New Zealand's chances in the World Cup.

For many years New Zealand cricket did not receive anything like the popular support given to the game in Australia. Public interest in the Saturday club competitions was cool. Many matches were played almost for the benefit of the players alone. The game as a whole was perpetually short of money. The best grounds were temporarily-converted rugby pitches. Rugby was the sport that attracted most New Zealanders. Maori, for some reason, have largely ignored the slower game. Iain Galloway is puzzled by this conspicuous absence of Maori from all levels of the game at a time when they are providing many international rugby players. "I have," he says, "discussed this with a number of my Maori friends. The answer I have been given is that their absence from cricket is largely based on social, and in the early days, political grounds. When we remember that the game was first played by the missionaries who came to convert Maori to Christianity and by British soldiers who came to fight them, it is not surprising that Maori regarded cricket as very much an English game played in long white trousers and shirts, by persons who should be treated with considerable suspicion – at best."

Martin Crowe, the captain of New Zealand, who was to prove for the duration of the series the best batsman in the world.

That New Zealand cricket is no longer the exclusive province of an amateurish middle-class and is no longer regarded as second-rate by the rest of the cricketing world is mainly due to the efforts of two great cricketers. The first was John Reid, magnificent attacking batsman and seam bowler, who dominated New Zealand cricket throughout the decades of the fifties and sixties, lifting standards in both islands to an extent where New Zealand started winning Test Matches. The other great player to make a huge difference was Richard Hadlee, who coming a generation after Reid became not only New Zealand's greatest bowler but one of the best fast bowlers in all cricket history.

But even when the team was well-balanced and well-organised, events beyond the Laws of Cricket occasionally intervened to ruin promising international tours. Vijay Rana tells the story of the disastrous 1987 tour of Sri Lanka:

> *The New Zealand team arrived in Colombo in April and fears were raised not only about the safety of the team, but also about the possibility of terrorist reprisals against the Test crowds. And this nearly happened. The violence escalated after the First Test, when approximately 400 people were killed in a week. The violence climaxed on April 21st with a massive bomb explosion in the centre of Colombo, which killed over 100 people. This was about 600 metres from the hotel where the New Zealand team was staying, to the shock of the players. Telephone enquiries from their families at home further depressed them, as Richard Hadlee recalled in his autobiography, Rhythm and Swing:*
>
> One of the players' wives rang and said that she didn't want to become a widow, and some of the Sri Lankan players also told us that we should go home.
>
> *Cricket had never seem anything like this before. Next morning Ken Dias, the New Zealand team manager, decided to return home. "Given the state of mind of the players," he said, "there is little point in continuing the tour. That is the inevitable conclusion."*

Despite these and other setbacks, great players flourished in the wake of Reid and Hadlee as never before in New Zealand – Turner, Coney, Crowe and others – to the extent that my all-time New Zealand XI measured up well to other national selections:

Turner	259
Sutcliffe	230
Dempster	136
Donnelly	206
Crowe	188
Reid	142
Hadlee	151
Wadsworth	80
Grimmett	50
Cowie	45
Collinge	68
TOTAL	1505

Bowling: Hadlee, Cowie, Collinge, Reid, Grimmett.

My Kiwi friend Trevor Chesterfield, who in many discussions heavily influenced this choice, took strong exception to the inclusion of Grimmett. Though a particular admirer of his fellow Kiwi-born idol, Trevor felt that Grimmett should have been bracketed with the country where he played all his important cricket, Australia, and that Alabaster should have been listed here in the legspinner's position. But I like the idea of cricketers representing the societies that produced them, which is why I included Ranjitsinjhi in the all-time Indian XI. Trevor and I both, however, regretted having to omit players like Vivian, Dacre, Coney, James, Pritchard, Dowling, Congdon and Wright. But the current New Zealand squad for the World Cup was a far cry from the above illustrious list, apart from the outstanding Martin Crowe.

Looking over the names of New Zealand's World Cup squad, I couldn't see any bowlers of consequence – certainly nobody to test the likes of Richie Richardson, Ian Botham and other positive batsmen. Would New Zealand ever get sides out? Would they get many wickets? And if they did, where was the batting in support of Crowe? Greatbatch had played no key role in the recently-concluded series against England, and Jones was about the best of a fairly ordinary-looking lot.

Here was New Zealand's likely team:

Wright
Latham
Jones
Crowe
Greatbatch
Rutherford
Smith
Morrison
Patel
Cairns
Watson

Bowling: Morrison, Watson, Cairns, Patel, Latham.

One massive advantage the New Zealanders would have would be the fact that all their matches except the final, if they reached it, would be played on their own New Zealand pitches. These notoriously slow pitches had undone many a great batsman used to quicker surfaces which encouraged strokeplay, and many a lively bowler, too, had been overcome with frustration on experiencing the anaesthetic effect of New Zealand pitches on bowling of pace.

Still, this was the country that had produced Sir Richard Hadlee, so if bowlers were fast enough and good enough they could presumably succeed in New Zealand.

At that stage I thought that if Greatbatch came off once or twice in support of Crowe, and if the Kiwi's held all their catches, they might conceivably win up to three of their matches through the hometown advantage factor. Presumably they could beat Zimbabwe and Sri Lanka, and maybe one of the others on a good day, given the breaks.

But, again, I couldn't see them reaching even the semi-final stage.

PAKISTAN

Eternal Divisions?

If this had been a tournament of Test Matches played over five days I would have ranked Pakistan as one of the main threats, even in the absence of Waqar Younis, but powerful though this team looked it seemed to me not to have the discipline and control for the one-day contest. Wasim Akram was a great strike bowler, as, no doubt, were the legspinners and Imran Khan himself, but the trend in one-day cricket was away from strike bowlers and towards containment, accuracy, frugality. Furthermore, it was being said that Imran Khan, owing to back strain, was to play more as a batsman and less as a bowler. And apart from the known greatness of Javed Miandad and Imran himself, the batting was largely an unknown quantity.

Imran raved about young Inzamam Ul-Haq, likening him to India's Tendulkar, but that sounded rather optimistic. Still, Pakistan had regularly produced cricketers of the highest order since the start of its cricket following partition from India in 1947.

Of all the great players for Pakistan, Abdul Qadir will always have a special place in my affections – as, no doubt, in the hearts of all those who, at one time or another,

How's that! Street scene in Karachi in 1978.

41

Bangladeshis demonstrate for the recognition of their country at Worcester during the 1971 tour of England by Pakistan.

have lamented the passing of leg spin bowling. Until Qadir emerged, it seemed that the wristy back-of-the-hand delivery was too hard to control and therefore too expensive in this era of limited-overs cricket.

It seems that Qadir could not be other than a leg spinner. He even walks like one between deliveries, with his feet apparently magnetized to the turf for preparatory purchase. He goes to the most complicated set of movements to begin his bowling action. He holds his left hand high as if in final salute to the doomed batsman, while his right hand twirls the ball urgently to appraise it of future rotational requirements, then squirts the ball into the upraised left hand while his feet begin a ritual dance on the spot. The left hand brandishes the ball momentarily, then transfers it back into the right, which is already beginning a series of small circular sweeps as he bounds and gambols into his curving approach run

In all this activity his entire body is the mere servant of the cocked right wrist as it sweeps over out of a flurry of wheeling arms to float the buzzing ball at his victim, and so complete in all bodily involvement that even after releasing the ball Qadir twirls after it up the pitch as if urging it on to work its own wickedness, and his bowling arm repeats an echo motion of the delivery to quench itself of every last vestige of spinfulness.

What the ball then does is variously astonishing. Taking on a life of its own, it loops and dips, pitching to spin vastly to left or right, or to spear straight on with top spin, and if it raps the batsman's pads, Qadir has a range of appeals for lbw – one supplicatory, one accusatory, one challenging and one slyly inquisitive, then the major one, the total, the ultimate appeal. With this he dances an angry tattoo upon the turf jumping up and down and uttering fierce cries of the sort that surely terrified whole generations of marauders clear out of the Khyber pass.

Both the superb art and the un-Anglo-Saxon appeals of Qadir are full of the spirit of Pakistan cricket. The traditions of cricket in Pakistan are those of the Muslim Indians

42

Jubilation among the crowd at Lahore when Pakistan were playing.

before partition. Whether true or not – and some historians of the Raj would strongly dispute it – Qamar Ahmed suggests that "it is common belief, that the partition of India and the creation of Pakistan was the direct result of the 'divide and rule' policy of the British Raj. This was felt to have not only divided India, but also the Indians. The seeds were believed to have been sown as early as Robert Clive's conquest of Bengal. Although both the Hindus and Muslims were involved in the uprising, the mutiny of 1857 was perceived to have turned the British against the Muslims. They felt themselves to be discriminated against in education, business and government. Tensions between Muslims and Hindus increased alongside hostility towards the Raj. These differences still existed in 1947 when India achieved Independence. The Muslim majority areas in the north-west, with the exception of Kashmir, and the north-east of the subcontinent were drawn out to form West and East Pakistan, separated by a thousand miles of Indian territory. The eastern wing of Pakistan, where cricket had not yet taken root, became Bangladesh."

Because Muslim cricketers had always featured in pre-partition Indian teams, Pakistan had a ready-made cricket culture, and, unlike any other cricket country, began its international participation on equal terms with other major countries, winning Test matches from the start. This had been a considerable achievement; full in the face of obstacles of every kind. "The partition of India and the creation of Pakistan (meaning 'The Land of the Pure')," writes Qamar Ahmed, "resulted in the death of thousands of people. Muslims, Hindus and Sikhs were all affected. Millions from both sides of the border were forced to migrate and begin life anew. refugees came from all walks of life, including cricketers. The Muslims had taken up cricket a little later than the Parsees and the Hindus but founded a Mohammedan Club in 1893 and were soon competing successfully in the annual Pentagular Tournament. However, this competition was felt to have created sectarian ill-feeling and polarised the religious communities of India at a time when they were involved in delicate negotiations towards the constitutional changes which led, eventually, to independence from the Raj. With Partition the established players of what became Pakistan were joined by Muslim cricketers from the South, the most outstanding of whom were the record-breaking Mohammad brothers, Hanif, Wazir, Raees, Mushtaq and Sadiq. They came from the state of Junagadh, leaving their

A section of the ladies stand at Karachi during England's tour in 1977, succumbing – as was later disapprovingly noted by Pakistani officials – to the excitement of Imran Khan's bowling.

home and all their material possessions behind. Junagadh is in the Kathiwar peninsula, an area that had an ancient cricket history boasting such names as Ranjitsinhji, Duleepsinhji, Amar Singh and Vinoo Mankad. With this tradition behind them and with all the determination to succeed which characterises the migrant, the Mohammad family dominated cricket – so much so, that for twenty-five years Pakistan never took the field without a Mohammad brother. Between them they scored 10,938 test runs, including twenty-nine centuries. In first class cricket they scored over 78,000 runs and took over 1200 wickets – by any standards, a remarkable achievement."

In Pakistan's first tour of England in 1954 they shared the series, winning the Oval Test. As Qamar Ahmed tells the story, "the MCC, encouraged by Pakistan's performance in India the year before, invited the team to England. During the wettest summer in memory, Pakistan were able to draw the four Test rubber, winning the final test by 24 runs against a team containing such illustrious names as Hutton, Compton, May, Graveney, Simpson, Statham and Loader. The architect of the victory was Pakistan's first outstanding bowler, Fazal Mahmood, who took twelve wickets. Pakistan thus gained the distinction of being the first country to have won a Test on their first trip to England."

Pakistan's cricketing relations with the other test-playing countries have not always been easy. Test matches with India are notorious for crowd disturbances, mutual abuse and over-defensive play on both sides. Difficulties have often centred around the questions of umpires. "It is," claims Qamar Ahmed, "to the credit of Pakistan that they became the first country to invite third-country umpires to supervise Test series at home – against the West Indies and India in 1986 and 1989. Both those series were played without the ill-feeling which had marred the series against England in 1987-8 – when, in the Faisalabad Test, Umpire Shakoor Rana and the England captain, Mike Gatting, had come near to blows."

Test teams from Pakistan had also suffered from a multitude of internal divisions. There sometimes seemed to be as many captains on the field as players. But the arrival of Imran Khan on the scene resolved these difficulties – to some considerable extent. Imran's commanding stature as a player, his considerable skills as a diplomat, and his no-nonsense approach to team selection on merit, have had a lot to do with Pakistan's recent success.

A prime example of this has been Imran's insistence on bringing young players without a great deal of experience into the national side – Waqar Younis and Wasim Akram are the two most striking examples of this. But overall, Pakistan's international record had been so impressive that selection of their all-time XI was almost an automatic process:

Hanif Mohammad	337
Sadiq Mohammad	166
Zaheer Abbas	274
Javed Miandad	280
Mushtaq Mohammad	201
Asif Iqbal	175
Imran Khan	136
Wasim Akram	123
Wasim Bari	85
Abdul Qadir	61
Waqar Younis	8
TOTAL	1856

Bowling: Waqar Younis, Wasim Akram, Imran Khan, Abdul Qadir, Asif Iqbal.

Omitted with regret were the great Fazal Mahmood, Intikhab Alam, Majid Khan and Saeed Ahmed, and it occurred to me only after compiling this list that three of those named were in Pakistan's 1992 World Cup squad – Imran Khan, Javed Miandad and Wasim Akram – and that Waqar Younis and Abdul Qadir would also have been in the squad if fit! An even stronger squad than I had thought, then, though I still had reservations about the untried middle order batting, and the ability of the bowlers to bowl accurately within the strict confines of the one-day formula. The probable team drawn from the squad was:

Ramiz Raja
Aamir Sohail
Imran Khan
Javed Miandad
Inzamam Ul-Haq
Salim Malik
Moin Khan
Wasim Akram
Mushtaq Ahmed
Aqib Javed
Akram Raza

Bowling: Wasim Akram, Aqib Javed, Imran Khan, Mushtaq Ahmed, Akram Raza

SRI LANKA

Cricket in a Time of Chaos

For various reasons I did not expect a great deal from Sri Lanka. Although they were always strong in batting, they seemed to be short of strong bowling especially of the strike variety. I expected them to play as well as could be hoped from a country that had experienced few Test matches and whose recent history off the field had been so disturbed.

For more than a decade, normal life in this "emerald isle" has been disrupted. Law and order has broken down, thousands have been killed, and hundreds of thousand forced to take refuge in foreign lands. When the moderate politics of the Tamil United Liberation Front surrendered to one of the most violent movements in modern history, the Liberation Tigers of Tamil Elem, violence became the political norm in Sri Lanka as it is in danger of becoming in South Africa.

And yet, astonishingly, cricket continues somehow amidst this political upheaval, but it has not, in Vijay Rana's opinion "flourished. Politicians in Colombo and Tamil extremists have between them contributed to the chaos of national cricket. Since the anti–Tamil riots of 1983, violence has been inseparable from politics, and politics inseparable from cricket."

Cricket, unfortunately, is not a force for national unity in Sri Lanka. "At national level," Vijay Rana points out, "it is dominated by the Singhalese, the Tamils having consistently felt they are discriminated against by the national selectors — who are mainly Singhalese. There have been Tamils representing Sri Lanka at top level, but never enough to satisfy the Tamil community. In 1975, London–based Tamil groups held a demonstration against the racial bias of the team when the Sri Lankans were playing at the Oval. Although the cricket authorities argue that the selection is made purely on merit, it is the Singhalese in and around Colombo in the south of the country that enjoy better cricket facilities and therefore have a better chance of getting into the team. Anyone living outside the main cities of Colombo, Kandy and Galle, whether Singhalese or Tamil, would have less chance of success than young players studying in the elite schools of the cities."

The abandonment of the 1987 tour by New Zealand seemed to be a death blow for international cricket in Sri Lanka. And yet more disappointments were to follow. In February 1988, the Australians decided to call off their tour, and later in July England, too, called off their six weeks visit because of the security problems. This unfortunate isolation did not come to an end until August 1992, when Allan Border's Australian team played three Test matches in Colombo, the only city in the cricket world to have three Test grounds.

"The fear of terrorist reprisals has discouraged foreign teams," laments Vijay Rana, "and local tournaments have aroused public anger. As the country continues to burn, some complain, the rich and powerful indulge in the Englishman's pursuit. These feelings are best summed up in a popular song – a mother's lament as her son was taken away by the security forces to be tortured and perhaps killed:

Tell me, what wrong did my son do,
When some young cynics from the school of the élite
Indulge in drink and dance, while playing cricket.
Is it wrong for my one and only son
Who saw his country on fire
To find ways to put it out."

The charge of elitism is, at least partly, justified. As in so many countries, cricket began in what is now Sri Lanka as the pastime of the elite – the English military rulers. The first reference to a cricket match played in the country is found in the November 3rd 1832 edition of the Colombo Journal, the only English newspaper of that time. "It was," Vijay Rana points out, "an all–England affair, mainly involving British soldiers. The first Ceylonese club, known as the Colts Club, was formed in 1873, and soon earned a reputation as the 'Invincible Colts'. It is surprising that the first match between the Europeans and the Ceylonese did not take place until fourteen years later, in 1887. From the battalions of the Army, and the clubs of the ruling elite, cricket spread slowly through schools and colleges to its natural roots in the people of the country. Part of the credit for this must go to Ashley Walker, later described as the 'father of Ceylonese

cricket', a Cambridge Blue and master at the Royal College, Colombo, where he passed on his love of the sport to the native boys at the college in the early years of this century."

Sri Lanka's geographical position on the routes to Australia exposed the country to some high class cricket. As Vijay Rana puts it: "on the long and boring journeys between Australia and England, the beautiful island provided a temptingly relaxing stop–over, which was even better when that could be combined with match practice. These casual journey-breaks by the English and Australian teams did much to popularise cricket. In 1882 an Englishman, George Vanderpar, first arranged for the Hon. Ivo Bligh's English team to play a 'whistle–stop' game in Colombo. But as they set sail on the Peshawar the ship collided with another just outside Colombo harbour. So they had to anchor again and play a second match against the Dublin Fusiliers. In 1914 the first Australian team to arrive in Sri Lanka was from New South

Aravinda De Silva, Sri Lanka's captain, and a batsman of such freedom that even Imran Khan was unable to contain him.

47

Wales, led by Rev. E. F. Waddy. They played in Colombo, Kandy, Galle and Anuradhoura. G. F. Vernon took the first English team on an extended tour of Sri Lanka in 1888 and the first MCC team arrived in 1927. Three years later Maharjkumar of Vizianagaram took an Indian team which included two guest cricketers from England, Jack Hobbs and Herbert Sutcliffe."

Sri Lanka made their presence felt internationally sixty years ago when, led by C.H.Gunasekera, they made their first overseas tour to India. In 1945 India reciprocated, and, four years later, the West Indians and Pakistanis visited Sri Lanka to play unofficial Tests. "Cricket," according to Vijay Rana, "was becoming immensely popular, and, even though there was no money in the game, national players were granted star status. Although cricket was being liberated from its elitist image, an expanding middle class became increasingly involved. Cricket was still viewed as an opportunity to climb the social ladder."

A new era of Sri Lankan cricket dawned when, under Tissera's captaincy, Sri Lanka defeated Pakistan's A team in 1964. In the same season, supported by Jayasinghe's remarkable batting, Tissera led Sri Lanka to a memorable victory against their giant neighbour, India, in the third unofficial Test in Ahmedabad.

By the early seventies, cricket had become a focus of mass enthusiasm. Tony Lewis remembers:

> I shall not forget the roar at the Colombo Oval when Geoff Boycott had his stumps shattered with the second ball of the innings in 1970. They reckoned that the noise of the crowd was so loud and prolonged that the coconuts fell off the trees up in Kandy.

It was not until a hundred and fifty years after the forming of the first cricket club that Sri Lanka attained Test status. In February 1982, Keith Fletcher's England cricket team arrived in Colombo to play the first official Test match. Vijay Rana tells the story:

> For the tired English cricketers it was just another Test on a hot and humid morning. Four months away from home, they had just lost a six Test series in India. The Indian captain, Sunil Gavaskar's defensive tactics had deprived them of the thrills of cricket, after they had lost the first Test of the series. And now, in this unknown land, described to tourists as 'Paradise Island', they were to make a new beginning.
>
> Sitting in the newly built commentary box of Colombo stadium were the BBC Radio commentators, Don Mosey, Henry Blofeld and Tony Lewis, swatting and moaning about the scorching sun.
>
> 'And Willis races in to bowl from the Cooling Tower End to Warnapura and Sri Lanka's Test history is about to begin.'
>
> For an emotionally overwhelmed Bandula Warnapura, the captain of Sri Lanka, it was a rare convergence of dream and reality, as he recalled:
>
> 'It was a dream for me which came true. I never knew when I started playing cricket whether I was going to be the first captain of Sri Lanka or the first person to face the first ball or get the first official run for Sri Lanka. So it was indeed a dream to me, which came true.'

In the very first Test against a team which had one of the most successful generation of cricketers — Boycott, Botham, Gower, Gooch, Emburey and Underwood — Sri Lankans displayed the qualities which in the coming years were to become the hallmark of their national cricket: sparkling brilliance devoid of professional consistency. It was, as

Vijay Rana recalls "a remarkable match. Warnapura, Wettimuny and Dias were back in the pavilion before the score reached thirty. Then two youngsters, Ranjan Madugalle (aged 22) and Arjuna Ranatunga (aged 19) salvaged the sinking ship by each getting over half a century. Derrick Underwood took five for 28 in 18 overs. Sri Lanka were out for 218. Then De Mel took four for 70, and De Silva three for 54 and thereby contained England who only managed a meagre lead of five runs. However in the second innings inexperienced Sri Lankans succumbed to Emburey, losing seven wickets for eight runs in eleven overs and three balls. Emburey emerged with figures of six for 33." It was not a particularly auspicious beginning. Both cricketing luck and the ravages of politics seemed to be conspiring against the game in Sri Lanka.

In September 1985, Sri Lanka won their first Test and the series against India. In the Colombo Test India lost by 149 runs. The Sri Lankans, tells Vijay Rana, "had carefully united their defence against an uninspiring attack led by the Indian skipper, Kapil Dev, with an innings of 385 — including a magnificent 111 runs by de Silva, 95 by Roy Dias and 50 by the captain Mendis. Though the Indian team suffered from their own infighting — North versus South, or Kapil Dev versus Gavaskar, they also accused the umpire S. Ponnadoral, the only Tamil on the field, of many doubtful umpiring decisions. Later Kapil Dev said angrily:

> ...the Sri Lankans were better in batting, bowling, fielding ... and umpiring. They will never win a Test match in any other country."

In fact, the defeat of India was a classic case of underrating a supposedly weak enemy. The Indian captain later admitted that his players came on the tour without sufficient preparation, and some players came straight from the English season — taking the Sri Lankan challenge very lightly.

Victory over India was a rare triumph for a troubled nation, something, Vijay Rana warns, "its public will now expect every time Mendis and his men stride onto a Test ground. The team was showered with messages of congratulations, and newspapers wrote inspiring editorials:

> 'They have given us all a lesson, not only in cricket but also in life, on how to face its trials, setbacks and challenges, its triumphs and disasters. May God give us more of such men.'

But even in this moment of glory the Sri Lankan captain, Duleep Mendis, was pondering the future:

> 'I hope they understand that Test cricket isn't easy and that we won't be expected to win every time'."

Sri Lanka is still not taken entirely seriously by the older cricketing nations. In their three official tours to England, Sri Lanka only played three Tests, and they have yet to play a five Test series anywhere in the world. But if not exactly a force for unity, cricket has rekindled national pride in Sri Lanka. As Vijay Rana puts it:

> Thousands of ordinary young children began to dream of becoming the Tisseras or De Silvas of the future, as they played cricket with a soft ball and piece of wood under the shadows of coconut trees on the world's most idyllic beaches.

And yet I couldn't see them beating some of the strong sides I had still to consider.

WEST INDIES

Hamlet Without the Prince?

I f there had been heavy conspiring up in the heavens for the great game of cricket to be conceived of there, down on earth was a ready-made supply of human beings ready to become the greatest natural cricketers on earth – the West Indians.

Mainly from Barbados, Trinidad, Jamaica, and Guyana, and lately Antigua, the brilliant cricketers from the Caribbean lifted the game to new heights in batting, fielding, fast bowling and spin and established an ascendancy for a whole generation in the seventies and eighties.

The history of West Indian cricket is encapsulated in the career of one of the greatest of all batsmen, George Alphonso Headley. "Headley", Hugh Crosskill reports, "was born in Panama on May 30th, 1909. His father was Barbadian and his mother Jamaican. Like thousands of other West Indians, Headley's parents had gone in search of greater fortune. At the time the Americans were building the Panama Canal to link the Pacific Ocean with the Caribbean sea, and wages were higher than those paid in the West Indian islands. George Headley was sent to Jamaica when his father and mother left Panama for Cuba. Soon, like thousands of other West Indian children, Headley was playing 'backyard cricket' at his new home in Kingston. Bats were shaped from coconut boughs and young breadfruits were used as balls. Sometimes the balls were made by wrapping a stone in cloth which was then bound with cords and black electrical tape. If this missile hit the shins it could be very painful, so youngsters soon became skilled in playing shots off their legs – more to do with self-preservation than style! After making his mark in club cricket, Headley was chosen to play against Lord Tennyson's touring team early in 1928. He made good use of the opportunity, scoring 211. In 1930 Headley was invited to join the West Indies squad in Barbados for the first Test against England. On January 11th, 1930, he won the first of his twenty-two Test caps. He was out for 21 in the first innings, but in the second he scored the first of his ten Test hundreds, a brilliant 176. For the next nine years Headley carried the fortunes of West Indian cricket almost single-handedly. In all he played twenty-two tests, scoring 2,190 runs, a top score of 270 and an average of just under 61. Sir Neville Cardus referred to Headley as the 'Black Bradman'. It was the sportswriter, Denzil Batchelor, who turned that remark around, to the satisfaction of the West Indians, by saying:

There are times when I think Bradman at his very best was fit to be called the white Headley."

By the nineteen-fifties the talent was more evenly spread in the West Indies team. Hugh Crosskill picks up the story: "History was created with the first ever series win in England, including the first ever triumph at Lords. It was a magnificently balanced team. Allan Rae and Jeff Stollmeyer, who both went on to become West Indies Board Presidents, formed a reliable opening partnership. Then came cricket's most famous triumvirate – the three W's – Clyde Walcott, Everton Weekes and Frank Worrell. Immortalised in calypso – "Those two little friends of mine, Ramadhin and Valentine!" – the spin twins, Sonny Ramadhin and Alf Valentine, mesmerised batsmen with their guile. Barbadian John Goddard, a fine off spinner, was the captain, and Gerry Gomez the hard working all rounder. By the time the team arrived there was already a sizeable West Indian population in England. Times were hard. The Motherland had not lived up to expectations and racism was prevalent. West Indians desperately needed to boost a sagging morale. The touring team provided just that. West Indians turned up at grounds in their thousands, bringing with them the carnival atmosphere of their homelands. When the West Indies scored that historic first win at Lords, calyspsonian Lord Kitchener and scores of other fans raced across the hallowed turf to serenade their heroes up on the balcony. The BBC commentator complained:

Never has such a sight been seen at Lords before."

That such sights were to be seen at Lords many times was largely due to one man and to a series of closely-connected international cricketing circumstances. As Hugh Crosskill puts it, "it took the 1974-75 series in Australia to fire West Indies cricket into life and to set the stage for a long period of world dominance. In that series the Australians used a four-pronged attack, spearheaded by Dennis Lillee and Jeff Thomson, two bowlers who had struck the fear of God into England the year before. They were fast and they were hostile. The West Indies crashed to a 5-1 defeat in the six-Test series.

England v West Indies, August 1973. The West Indies had, as usual, won comfortably. The crown obviously felt that the ball in the hands of their bowlers was more of a serious threat than the hoax bomb which had been a news item on the Saturday.

Batsmen of the calibre of Fredericks, Rowe and Kallicharran were left battered, bruised and bewildered. West Indian batsmen pride themselves on not being hit by opposing bowlers, but they had never before encountered pace of the kind generated by Lillee and Thomson on the hard, bouncy wickets of Australia. Clive Lloyd, the captain, left that series determined never to let that happen again."

In 1976 the West Indies were hosts to India in a Test Series. The first and second matches had been closely fought with the West Indies generally in the commanding position. The third Test was played at Port of Spain. Lloyd's team scored 359. India were bowled out in the first innings for 271. Lloyd declared the West Indies second innings closed at 271 – leaving India an impossible 406 runs to save the match in the remaining day and a half. But, thanks to some superb batting from Gavaskar (102) and Viswanath (112), India became the first team to chase such a total and win.

Lloyd attributed this astonishing defeat to the fact that he had been persuaded to play three spin bowlers – bowlers who had let him down. "With that," wrote Trevor McDonald in his authorised biography of Clive Lloyd, "the new Clive Lloyd philosophy about the use of fast bowlers was born. Back in the seventh century the Greeks initiated the idea of using heavily armed soldiers fighting in closed ranks, known as the phalanx. Lloyd initiated the idea that with four fast bowlers in his team they could be used as shock troops."

The Lloyd phalanx went into immediate battle in the fourth and final Test of the series at Sabina Park in Jamaica. Mihir Bose tells the story in his *A History of Indian Cricket*, claiming that "the West Indians started what the Indians thought was an unfair, 'barbaric', war against their batsmen. Three, Gaekwad, Viswanath and Patel, were sent to hospital. Holding was going round the wicket to bowl bouncers and the odd beamer. Viswanath had his middle finger broken. Gaekwad was hit on the temple and was in hospital for three days. Patel was hit on the lips by a short ball from Holder. Holding, who could look like an angel when running in to bowl, now seemed Dracula incarnate." When the series was over, Sunil Gavaskar wrote in his Book *Sunny Days*:

> *When I faced Holding, I received four bouncers in an over and a beamer which Holding had pretended had slipped from his hand ... After one over, I asked the umpire for his definition of intimidatory bowling. To call a crowd 'a crowd' in Jamaica is a misnomer. It should be called a mob. The way they shrieked and howled every time Holding bowled was positively horrible. They encouraged him with shouts of 'Kill him Maan!', 'Hit him Maan!', 'Knock his head off Mike!' All this proved beyond a shadow of a doubt that these people still belong to the jungles and forests instead of a civilised country.*

In the second innings seven Indian batsmen were described as 'absent hurt'.

The next West Indian Test series was against England, captained by South African Tony Greig who made a remark on television that English cricketers have been ruing ever since. He was asked his opinion on the outcome of the forthcoming tour. "In a fashion which," writes Trevor McDonald, "was typical of his extravagance, Greig replied that it was the intention of the England team to make the West Indies 'grovel'. It is a comment on his lack of sensitivity that to this day his former colleagues and friends insist that it never occurred to Tony Greig that for a white South African to talk about making a black West Indian team 'grovel' was about the nearest one could come to a

The Fifth Test between England and West Indies at the Oval in 1984.

formal declaration of the start of World War Three. That was certainly the way Greig's remarks were interpreted by the West Indies. And they resolved to punish him."

The West Indians have been punishing English cricketers ever since. Lloyd, as Hugh Crosskill puts it, "was to reign over a golden age of Caribbean cricket, during which he built what was arguably the finest team the game has ever seen." The fast-bowling phalanx consisted of Andy Roberts, Michael Holding, Colin Croft, Joel Garner, Malcolm Marshall, and Wayne Daniel – providing , as Hugh Crosskill says, "the proverbial pace like fire. In Greenidge and Haynes he had the most successful opening partnership in Test history. They were backed up by the brilliance of Viv Richards, Lawrence Rowe, Larry Gomes, Jeff Dujon and Lloyd himself. He led them to victory in the first two World Cup finals and in 1984 created another bit of history when the West Indies crushed England 5-0 in the Test series, The English press called it a 'whitewash', but for Caribbean fans it was clearly a 'blackwash'!"

Picking the West Indian all-time eleven needed, therefore, little research, nor was much consideration necessary to flick the eye over the following line-up and conclude that this was surely one of the strongest sides imaginable. The batting went down to number seven (imagine a team with Learie Constantine at seven!) and the bowling included some of the greatest fast bowlers and spinners in history. It was truly a formidable list:

Headley	270
Worrell	261
Weekes	207
Walcott	220
Richards	291
Sobers	365
Constantine	90
Holding	73
Hall	50
Ramadhin	44
Valentine	14
TOTAL	1885

Bowling: Holding, Hall, Constantine, Sobers, Ramadhin, Valentine and Worrell.

Two captains who lead from the front, sharing a joke: Viv Richards and Graham Gooch during the England v West Indies Test in 1991.

Two of the West Indian all-time greats, Headley and Sobers, were automatic choices for an all-time World XI, and as with the other great national sides, their strength could be gauged as well through the stars regretfully omitted, including Hunte, Nurse, Kanhai, Kallicharran, Greenidge, Marshall, Martindale, Garner, Sealy, Haynes and Goddard.

The amazing strength of West Indian cricket could also be gauged by considering a possible team selected only from the tiny island of Barbados.

It could probably have beaten any other complete national side on its day: Greenidge, Haynes, Worrell, Weekes, Walcott, Sobers, Goddard, Marshall, Martindale, Hall, Garner.

Yet the West Indies squad for the 1992 World Cup looked strangely tame to me ... Of course no team with such great players as Richie Richardson, Ambrose (probably the world's best batsman and bowler right there) Brian Lara, Gus Logie and Carl Hooper could be other than strong. Yet somehow there was not the depth and the brilliance all the way through that modern West Indies teams seemed to have as of right...

Marshall was past his best, Patterson was better suited to the five-day game and others like Cummins and Benjamin were as yet largely untested. Still, being West Indians, they would take a lot of beating and I expected them to reach the semi-final.

The most extraordinary omission from the squad was the great Viv Richards, who had indicated he was available. As Hugh Crosskill says; "Like so many of the great West Indian players of the past, Richards' international career ended on a sour note. After the 1991 series in England he announced his retirement from Test cricket, but made it clear that he would like to end his career with his fifth and final World Cup campaign. The selectors weren't interested and Richards was left to end his playing days with Glamorgan in the English county championship."

Over the years Hugh Crosskill has had many cricketing conversations with this proud Antiguan. "There are," he says, "fires burning within him that are likely to remain unextinguished for the rest of his life. He is a strong believer in black pride and the breaking down of the class barriers that still exist in the region. He also has strong sympathy with the Rastafarian movement, symbolised by the almost ever-present red, gold and green wristband. Richards plans to enter Antiguan politics when he finally hangs up his massive bat, following the tradition of cricketers-turned-politicians like Wes Hall and Roy Fredericks."

But the West Indian selectors opted instead for youth, and with Richards passed over by West Indies and David Gower passed over by England others could only wonder. Probably both Gower and Richards would have been snapped up by any other national team in the tournament. Still, the West Indian line-up was, as always, impressive:

Haynes
Lara
Richardson
Arthurton
Logie
Hooper
Williams
Marshall
Harper
Patterson
Ambrose

Bowling: Ambrose, Patterson, Marshall, Harper, Hooper.

A thoughtful Richie Richardson.

Viv Richards at Lords in 1978.

ZIMBABWE

A Nation of Gentlemen

Although they had many strengths, particularly in the field, I did not expect Zimbabwe, young as it was in cricketing terms, to make much of an impression in the 1992 World Cup. While they were always capable of causing an upset such as when they beat Australia in the 1983 World Cup, I did not think they had the depth of resources to call on nor the bowling attack to bring consistent wins,

From 1904 until 1979 Southern Rhodesia played cricket in the South African Currie Cup Competition under three ddifferent names: "Southern Rhodesia" up until 1965, "Rhodesia" until 1979 when it became known by the somewhat long-winded and transitory name of "Rhodesia-Zimbabwe". Finally in 1980 the country became known, simply, as "Zimbabwe".

With Independence cricket links with South Africa were broken and Zimbabwe had to go it alone in the world of cricket with about as many first class players in the whole country as most of the major English counties have on their books.

As Bob Nixon puts it, "in 1980 the big question was – where now for little Zimbabwe as a cricketing nation? One Government Minister was on record as saying that they would let cricket die since it was a 'white man's game' with little appeal to the African. However, two men (with their helpers) had been working hard before Independence on that very problem. Alwyn Pichanick, the President of the Zimbabwe Cricket Union is a lawyer. He is quiet and self-effacing and a born diplomat. David Ellman-Brown, the Vice-President, is more outgoing and exhaustingly energetic. Both men were determined not to let the game they loved become a mere memory in the new country."

The first target was to gain recognition as an Associate Member of the International Cricket Council. This was achieved on 23 July 1981. Zimbabwe could enter the ICC Trophy Competition in 1982. Victory would earn them a place in the World Cup to be held in 1983 in England. In the meantime Pichanick and Ellman-Brown arranged for at least two touring sides a year from all over the world to come for short tours – a few First Class and several one-day games.

In 1982 Zimbabwe won the ICC Trophy Competition, beating Bermuda at Leicester in England. Zimbabwe was a World Cup nation at last!

Bob Nixon tells the story of the first match of the 1982 Series:

The first match was against the mighty Australians on the ninth of June – General Election day in the United Kingdom – at Trent Bridge. I joined Henry Blofeld, Peter Parfitt and Fred Titmus in the Commentary Box, finding it difficult to convince myself that I was not dreaming. At the end of a day of great cricket, Zimbabwe set the competition alight by beating Australia by 13 runs. Victory was achieved by superb fielding – including some unbelievable catches. Australia had lost to a side of amateurs who believed that, if they put in a hundred per cent effort, any side in the world could be upset.

Zimbabwe never quite reached those dizzy heights again but they did well in all the remaining matches – except that against the West Indians which turned out to be, as Bob Nixon puts it, "the slaughter of the innocents". Zimbabwe returned home having beaten the mighty Australia, won two Man of the Match awards, and earned the reputation (on no lesser authority than Brian Johnston's) of being the best fielding side in the series.

In 1985 Zimbabwean cricket found, as Bob Nixon says "an unexpected ally":

One genuine and knowledgeable fan stated "Cricket civilizes people and creates good gentlemen. I want everyone in Zimbabwe to play cricket. I want ours to be a nation of gentlemen." The man responsible for these words is Robert Gabriel Mugabe – the President of Zimbabwe. Messers. Pichanick and Ellman-Brown were no longer fighting a lone battle for cricket in Zimbabwe.

Zimbabwe retained the ICC Trophy in England in 1986 (and so qualified for the next World Cup) with relative ease – despite being given "a real fright" by the Netherlands at Lords in a match which was won by only twenty-five runs. That series was played in India and Pakistan. Zimbabwe almost upset the applecart again in their very first match, by winning against New Zealand at Hyderabad, but the remaining matches were lost by considerable margins. Nevertheless the team returned home with the knowledge that, as Bob Nixon puts it, "they had, yet again, amazed everyone with their fielding".

The ICC trophy was retained once again in the Netherlands three years later – with some aplomb since the Netherlands were defeated in the final by six wickets. Zimbabwe were coming to Australia and New Zealand with a relatively unchanged squad. Eddo Brandes was to be their major strike bowler. It seemed to me that while Zimbabwe might be capable of surprising any unwary team they were unlikely to win many matches.

SOUTH AFRICA
The Prodigal Returns

I had left South Africa until last in my analyses of the national teams and their countries' place in the history and structure of world cricket, partly for sentimental reasons as I was born in South Africa and had felt involved with South African cricket since childhood, partly because I expected they would have a strong team quite capable of winning the World Cup – and I expected them to reach at least the semi-final stage – and partly because their presence in this tournament completed again the international cricket family, making the 1992 World Cup the most representative in history.

So there was my fourth predicted semi-finalist team, South Africa, to join England, Australia, Pakistan and West Indies. The television screen in the Qantas jumbo was now showing us nearing the end of our long flight from Tahiti. We were barely an hour out from Sydney, but in thought I was back in 1951, my final year of High School in Kimberley, aged 17.

Then as now every South African schoolboy cricketer aspired to play Nuffield cricket, the national championship for schoolboys in which teams were chosen to represent the

An anti-apartheid and anti-Gatting demonstration before the NatWest final at Lords in 1989.

58

sports provinces, and I was no exception.

The final trial match for our province, Griqualand West, was the key match between my school, Christian Brothers' College, and our strongest rivals, Kimberley High School. CBC and KHS, the two most famous schools of the region, were rivals in everything, not least in the numbers of Springbok cricketers each had produced. Shortly before, in South Africa's Test series in England in 1947, KHS had contributed Ken Viljoen and we had contributed Tony Harris – who was also a Springbok rugby flyhalf.

On that hot summer day in 1951 it was not only the final opportunity to impress the Nuffield selectors but also the crunch match against the arch-rivals, and the schools by tradition included the school professional in each team. KHS had a wily Welsh left-arm spin bowler named Emrys Davies, from Glamorgan, and we had an Australian pace bowler, Des Fitzmaurice, who had recently opened the bowling for Victoria with Bill Johnston.

I was one of the candidates for one vacancy still to be filled in the Nuffield team, that of opening batsman, and my main rival was the KHS opener, Jasper Streak, so the ideal scenario was obviously for me to do well and Streak to do badly ... but things hadn't started too well for me.

We batted first and instead of facing familiar pace I found I was shaping up to the dreaded Emrys Davies, who was actually taking the new ball, and the first four balls beat me embarrassingly. I thought the first was an off-break, but it was a "Chinaman", and I proceeded to misread the next three completely, not even managing to lay a bat on them.

In desperation I ran at the fifth to get it before it landed and he, adjusting quickly, dug it in shorter. I swung through the line, but he had cut it away to deceive me yet again, and my intended lofted on-drive became a grotesquely sliced off-drive. Still, there was enough bat on it to send it over mid-off for four, and from then on all went well as confidence grew, and I ended up with 44 runs.

We reached a fair total, then it was our turn to field – and my rival, Jasper Streak, now had to face up to our professional, Des Fitzmaurice. Our pro gave me a reassuring wink before starting his long run-up, and from slip I saw his first two outswingers beat the bat's edge and his third swing right in and neatly remove my rival's middle stump, sending it flying end over end. He was out and I was in the Nuffield team.

Four decades later, reliving the excitement, I can still see that beautiful fast inswinger from "Des Fitz"; can still hear his ripe Australian accent as he turned to me and growled: "Y'owe me a beer for that one, son!"

There were no intimations of mortality in those days. The bright sun on the green grass, with a cloudless sky of deep blue, gave everything the sense of permanence. I remember scoring exactly 44 because at the same time, six thousand miles away at Murrayfield in Edinburgh, the rugby Springboks had beaten Scotland 44 – 0, at that time a record score, and under the old points-scoring system too, with only three for a try. One wry old Scots fan had commented: "Aye, and we wurr lucky tae get the nil!"

Even earlier memories crowd in, of holidays at our Wild Coast cottage in the Transkei, of straining with my father and brother to hear through the crackle of static over the radio the distant commentary of John Arlott or Charles Fortune. In those days so much depended on so few – Bruce Mitchell, Dudley Nourse, Alan Melville. Once they went, it seemed, South Africa were in trouble. And in the tour of 1947 we were constantly suffering at the hands of twin scourges – Compton and Edrich.

Like other white kids of my generation in South Africa I was brought up as a racist and never thought to question white privilege. I only started turning against the system when I was at university in Cape Town, studying Law, though this did not mean I opposed South Africa's participation in international sport. I favoured the continuation of tours on the basis that they were "bridge-building" and would help to open minds in South Africa, and as recently as 1960 while visiting London I berated a group of demonstrators at Lord's – criticising them for picketing the Springbok cricketers not one of whom, I emphasised, was a supporter of the governing National Party nor an upholder of apartheid.

"These are sportsmen, not politicians!" I declared.

It was deeply embarrassing shortly thereafter when Jackie McGlew not only joined the National Party, thereby endorsing apartheid, but stood for parliament for it!

That was the start of my disillusion with the doctrine of "keeping politics separate from sport" – a lunatic view in retrospect, since sport is a part of life, and all life is connected to politics.

In 1968, with England about to tour South Africa and controversy raging about whether Basil D'Oliveira, a "coloured" South African, would be allowed to tour if chosen for England, I had, as a newspaper editor, an annual interview with the Prime Minister.

In it I gained the impression from Vorster that if D'Oliveira were chosen he would be allowed to tour on the basis that a refusal would generate bad publicity for South Africa at a time when the government was preparing to withstand campaigns abroad for economic sanctions against the apartheid policy. A key to it, in Vorster's view, was the firmness of the MCC and the British government. "Hulle moet maar besluit," he said. ("It is their decision"). He added that his own, Vorster's, position would be made easier in domestic political terms if Springbok cricketers backed D'Oliveira's inclusion, indicating their willingness to play against him. This seemed shrewd politics. The Springboks, as national heroes, carried a lot of weight with the public, and their lead would make Vorster's assent more palatable with his own party followers.

A few days later I was invited as vice-president of the Buffalo Cricket Club to be the main speaker at the club's centenary dinner at which all the Springbok cricketers would be present. In the course of my speech I said the Springbok cricketers could help resolve the D'Oliveira affair if they came out publicly in support of playing against him if he were chosen, adding that this would probably help Vorster to back the tour.

There was an immediate storm of booing and protest, amid shouts of: "Don't drag politics into sport!" Two of the Springbok cricketers walked out in protest – or so I was told at the time (it was later denied by them). When I eventually finished the speech there was a fresh outbreak of anger and the formal banquet ended in some disarray, especially when I said specifically to the Springbok cricketers: "If you don't act now, you may never play Test cricket again. If South African sportsmen don't speak up, South African sport may become isolated for many years."

The speech proved more prophetic than I realised at the time, and the only Springbok cricketer who pursued the matter with me was the captain, Trevor Goddard, who said he regretted what had happened but that the cricketers couldn't come out publicly on such a political issue.

"We're in a very difficult position," he said.

"No, Trevor, you're not," I said. "You are national heroes, nobody's going to put you in prison or on Robben Island. Besides, Vorster himself said it would help."

"Well, I see what you mean, but we really are in a very difficult position," he said.

I remember being filled with a sense of despair. Trevor Goddard was such a decent man, such a sterling character, that if he couldn't see the moral imperative I feared none of our Springbok cricketers would.

In the event, of course, D'Oliveira was inexplicably omitted from the original touring team. Only after prolonged controversy was his name added to the side – which gave Vorster the impression that neither MCC nor the British government were firm on the issue. The decision was announced in London coincidentally with the Orange Free State congress of the National Party, the most right-wing in the land, and Vorster acted the strong man for his followers and banned the tour.

Possibly to his surprise, the MCC did stand firm at last, and that was the end of South African touring cricket teams for almost a quarter-century.

Springbok cricketers did protest publicly against apartheid in sport when, in a well-planned gesture, they walked off the field at Newlands to issue a statement affirming their support for non-racial sport, but unfortunately this was three years later and, by then, the damage was irreparably done. By that time, too, the issue was no longer simply apartheid in sport, it was apartheid in all its manifestations.

Domestically the campaign to integrate cricket began in earnest, though it was limited to three centres – Pietermaritzburg in Natal, Green Point in Cape Town, and East London where I lived. By 1975 I had joined the non-racial South African Cricket Board of Control, which opposed tours and called for a moratorium on international sport until apartheid was abolished, and as the only white member of its seventeen-man executive council I was approached by South Africa's Minister of Sport, Dr. Piet Koornhof.

Koornhof was the ultimate pragmatist. A former Secretary-General of the Broederbond – the secret Afrikaner society which acted as the government's think-tank on policy matters – he had attended Oxford University and was markedly less doctrinaire than other members of the cabinet on apartheid matters.

He told me in private that he was convinced that apartheid in sport would have to go, but that he couldn't get the rest of the cabinet to agree. He asked if I would organise a meeting for him and the white cricket administrators to talk to SACBOC board members with a view to negotiating the end of cricket apartheid in such a way that the cabinet conservatives would see obvious benefits for the country, such as tours resulting.

But first he needed access to the black administrators, and so far they hadn't been prepared to meet him. Could I arrange this? "They don't trust me, you see, but they trust you," he said.

The meeting was duly arranged, but an early setback was that the white administrators refused to have me in the room because I was a journalist. It was explained that I was there as a SACBOC official, not as a journalist, but that didn't satisfy them.

At this the black delegates of SACBOC said they would withdraw since they were only prepared to attend if I was in their delegation. At this point, with Koornhof leaning on them, the white administrators agreed and the historic meeting began. This was the first of several tentative meetings over the years between the white cricket officials and the non-racial body, though full unity was still fifteen years off.

Meanwhile Kemal Casoojee, my SACBOC friend and fellow-delegate from Border, our sports province centred on East London, thought up a good scheme to challenge the segregated status quo. We started a new non-racial cricket club, but with a team deliberately chosen to reflect racial diversity – consisting of three whites, three blacks, three "coloureds" and two "Indians". Unsubtly, we called it the Rainbow Cricket Club, and we announced that it would be entered in the official Border League.

At that time Security Police officers were taking the names of cricketers who even attended multiracial net practices, so the expectation was that they would interrupt multiracial matches and arrest all those on the field. That, at any rate, was the fear of the white officials when we challenged them to let their teams play against Rainbow in the league. Their chairman, Lee Warren, kept saying: "We will not break the law!"

I spoke to Minister Koornhof, who said on the phone: "Ach, man, just tell Warren to go ahead and play your chaps without any fuss. As long as there's no publicity I guarantee the Security Police won't make arrests."

But Lee Warren wouldn't accept that. "How do we know you really spoke to the Minister of Sport?" he said. "We want the Minister's permission in writing."

I flew to Johannesburg and went to see Dr. Koornhof, who had with him his top civil servant, a highly conservative official named Dr. Beyers Hoek. When I explained that Lee Warren and his colleagues insisted on the Minister putting his permission to play multiracial cricket in writing, Dr. Koornhof threw his hands up in the air. "Are they mad? How long do they think I'd last in Mr Vorster's government if I put a thing like that in writing, on my ministerial letterhead? I'd be thrown out of the blerry government, man!"

"Well, Dr. Koornhof, " I ventured. "They didn't say anything about an official letterhead, they just said 'in writing'." I took out a cigarette packet from my pocket and scrawled out written ministerial permission for the Rainbow Cricket Club to compete in the Border League, and invited Koornhof to sign it.

Dr. Beyers Hoek was beside himself with dismay. Plucking at Koornhof's sleeve, he was whispering that such a thing was out of the question – but Koornhof was smiling, clearly intrigued at the idea of something in writing not being something officially in writing ... He reached out for the packet – Peter Stuyvesant Filter-tip 30 – and began to chuckle. Dr. Beyers Hoek was whispering very fast and very loudly into his ear, but Dr. Koornhof brushed his arguments aside: "Ach, Beyers, we've got to blerry start somewhere ..." and he signed the cigarette packet.

And that's how we integrated cricket in Border province!

Fourteen years later in Washington D.C., where Dr. Koornhof was South African Ambassador to the United States, only three weeks after Mandela's release from prison and my own unbanning, we met for a reunion drink and spoke about the fateful cigarette packet. "I've still got it among my papers," I told him. "One day I'll donate it to the South African cricket archives."

Following the incident of the signed cigarette packet, I attempted some bridge-building activities at Koornhof's request which included plans for getting the white rugby administrators, led by Dr. Danie Craven, together with the non-racial groups under the South African Rugby Union, with a view to eventual union. At the time the non-racial group, headquartered in Port Elizabeth, had more than two hundred thousand

The ferocious strike bowling of South Africa's Allan Donald.

playing affiliates – mostly black schoolchildren – and only seven white members. I was one of these seven, but the most famous were the remarkable Watson brothers and their father, who defied police and government threats and had their house burned down by right-wing elements for playing rugby in the townships for Kwazakhele Club.

In July 1977 I travelled to Europe as delegate of the South African Chess Federation to the International Chess Federation and made a side trip to London to see Peter Hain and the South African Non-Racial Olympic Committee members with a message from Koornhof proposing some sort of negotiations to end sports apartheid.

Sam Ramsamy, who led the long campaign against apartheid sport, and Dennis Brutus, who had founded SANROC, were there along with Peter Hain and Chris de Broglio. They decided on a "wait-and-see" policy to test Koornhof's real intentions. I was given a return message to deliver to Koornhof.

Shortly after these first faltering steps by the South African government to respond to the sports boycott with concessions, in which I was the unlikely messenger for both sides, my friend Steve Biko was killed in Security Police detention, and for helping to raise an outcry over his death I was arrested and banned by the South African government. I later learnt that Dr. Koornhof had tried to talk his cabinet colleagues out of this action, but that they had chosen to follow the urgings of the Minister of Police, Mr J.T.Kruger, who considered me "a danger to the stability of the nation." Confined to a form of house detention and forbidden to communicate publicly, I was effectively isolated from many friends and colleagues, although one famous cricketer, André Bruyns, went out of his way to show his support for my position.

André, who would probably have been Springbok cricket captain if South African cricket hadn't been isolated, openly visited me in my house knowing that the Security Police were noting his car licence number. André, in fact, was one of the first elements of an exciting new development in South African cricket – the increasing emergence of young Afrikaners on the national cricket scene.

But under banning orders I was unable to function further on the sports negotiation front, and in fact three months later I escaped from my watchers in disguise, reached the Lesotho border, was joined by my wife and five children there and flew with them to London where I was given political asylum by the British government.

In the twelve years since going into exile in January 1978 I joined the international campaign to isolate South African sport and worked closely with Sam Ramsamy, Peter Hain, Chris de Broglio and Dennis Brutus to intensify all the external pressures that could be brought to bear to hasten the demise of the apartheid system.

Unfortunately the white South African cricket authorities, instead of undertaking serious steps to get significantly closer to the black administrators and to show readiness to follow their lead, embarked on a policy of arranging rebel tours to bypass the boycott.

It made sense if they were thinking primarily of white cricket and only in the short term, but it enraged and further estranged the very people they needed to get closer to – their black South African compatriots.

The last straw, the final affront to blacks by the white cricket administrators, was the Gatting tour of 1990 – although, ironically, the uproar it caused in South Africa caused the white administrators, such as Dr. Ali Bacher, to realise for the first time the extent of black feeling about such ventures.

This realisation by Bacher and his colleagues, and the trust that consequently began to build up between them and the sports representatives of the ANC such as Steve Tshwete, led directly to the uniting of the various factions in cricket administration in South Africa and also led ultimately to South Africa's participation in the 1992 World Cup.

Unlike New Zealand and some of the other cricket countries, South Africa had enjoyed success in international cricket as far back as the turn of the century, beating England on several occasions and winning series both at home and abroad. There had been glorious tours such as the tour of the four googly bowlers – Schwarz, Vogler, Faulkner and White – and later in 1935 when South Africa won the series in England thanks to another googly bowler, Zenophon Balaskas. But after both world wars South African cricket had suffered. In World War Two South Africa had contributed the largest volunteer army in the world against Hitler, only to have ex-servicemen discriminated against by the new Afrikaner Nationalist government which took power on a promise to institute a system of racial discrimination called apartheid.

What had always hampered South African cricket was not only that it was a game of the white minority, but that it was a game of the English-speaking minority of the white minority. Whites constituted only 15%, and only 38% of white South Africans were English-speakers, mainly of British descent. The 62% majority of whites were Afrikaners, mainly of Dutch descent, few of whom traditionally showed any interest in cricket.

Yet in spite of being a minority of a minority, English-speaking white South Africans produced, over the first seventy years of the twentieth century, some of the greatest cricketers in history. In their last nine Test Matches against Australia, in 1966 and 1970, South Africa drew one, lost one and won seven.

Among their world-class players were Horace "Jock" Cameron, reckoned by his contemporaries the world's greatest wicketkeeper, especially in speed of stumping. Wally Hammond described how Cameron stood up to medium-fast bowling and stumped batsmen one-handed from wide of the crease – including Hammond himself on two occasions. Cameron was also one of the finest attacking batsmen since England's great Gilbert Jessop. His most famous innings was a fast 90 in the Lord's Test of 1935, in which he captained South Africa to victory.

He had also hit a whirlwind 170 against Yorkshire in that year, hitting Hedley Verity for three fours and three sixes in one over and prompting the immortal line from Yorkshire's own wicketkeeper, Arthur Wood: "Tha hast him in two minds, Hedley – he doesn't know whether to hit thee for four or for six." Cameron had died tragically young of enteric fever shortly after that triumphant tour.

Another world-class player from South Africa was Aubrey Faulkner, not only the finest leg spin-googly bowler of his time but the country's leading batsman as well. In the season of 1909 he headed the batting against England with an average of 60.55, and had bowling figures of 29 wickets at 21.89 each, and in 1911 against Australia in Melbourne he hit a brilliant 206.

The two great South African batsmen of the early years were the giant Jimmy Sinclair, who hit South Africa's fastest Test century (in 80 Minutes) against Australia in Cape Town in 1902 after hitting 106 against Lord Hawke's England team three years earlier, and Herby Taylor, who was said to be the only batsman the great S.F. Barnes refused to bowl against. Against Barnes on the 1913 England tour of South Africa Taylor scored innings of 109, 91 and 83 not out in the Tests, and 100, 91 and 83 not out in provincial matches. Barnes, though, took 49 wickets in four Tests! Taylor was particularly renowned for his footwork and spectators sometimes observed that he played back so far that his back foot was on occasion several inches behind the off-stump or leg-stump, his "feel" for where the stumps were in relation to his feet being phenomenal. Taylor also had such a precise sense of the ball's trajectory that his method of letting a ball go was to turn the blade of the bat at the last instant, teasing the bowler with a near-stroke.

It might have been this irritating habit that caused Barnes to refuse to bowl to him, if not throw the ball down on the ground at the time as the legend originally had it – a version Barnes strenuously denied. Herby Taylor's greatness was such that his international career spanned twenty years, some being lost to war and illness, and in that time he scored slightly under 3000 Test runs at an average of over 40. His final tour was to Australia and New Zealand in 1931 at the age of 41, as a generous gesture to the South African cricket authorities in accompanying a young and inexperienced team, when he scored 78 and 84 in the Adelaide Test. It had the Australian players spontaneously applauding the beauty and command of his strokeplay, acknowledging

Kepler Wessels, the South African captain

why his reputation for greatness had preceded him.

Between the two World Wars the towering figure of South African cricket was Dudley Nourse, whose father had also played for South Africa, participating in South Africa's first Test victory over England. Dudley Nourse's greatest innings was his 231 in the second Test in Johannesburg against an Australian attack including Grimmett, O'Reilly and Fleetwood-Smith.

Wars took a heavier toll of South African Test cricketers than of Test players from any other country. The First World War cost the lives of three Test players from England, two from Australia and one from New Zealand but no fewer than six from South Africa, including two of the great googly exponents – Schwarz and White. In the Second World War South Africa lost Doolie Briscoe and Chud Langton from its successful 1938 Test team.

But South African cricket had a greater enemy than world war – it was racism. Long before the official apartheid system of 317 racial laws was initiated legislatively in 1948, South African teams were chosen on a racial basis. The country's best fast bowler, Hendriks, was left out of a touring team at the turn of the century because he was "coloured".

Three decades later an English friend sought to introduce the white South African, Blanckenberg, to Learie Constantine in a Lancashire League dressing-room, but the South African refused to shake hands with a black man. The incident reverberated to distant parts of the world, not least the Caribbean, where a particular hostility to South African racism developed over the years. But how good were the South Africans after all the years in exile? How would they shape up in the World Cup? I had never seen most of them play, and relied on the opinions of friends for estimates of their ability. What was clear right from the start was that we had no pretenders in the squad to the crowns of Barry Richards and Graeme Pollock.

This, however, was not necessarily an indictment, since countries only produced the likes of Pollock and Richards once in a half-century or so. Without any question Graeme Pollock had proved himself the greatest batsman in South African cricket history and one of the greatest of any era. Although he played in only 23 Tests before the boycott descended, he had an aggregate of 2256 and an average of over 60. Only marginally behind him in brilliance was Barry Richards, who suffered even more from the boycott in that it began almost coincidentally with the start of Richards' career in Tests. The same applied to the great fast-bowling all-rounder, Mike Procter. Nevertheless, enough was known of these brilliant cricketers to include them in the all-time South African XI:

Rowan	236
Richards	140
Taylor	176
Nourse	231
Pollock	274
Sinclair	106
Faulkner	204
Cameron	90
Procter	48
Tayfield	75
Adcock	24
TOTAL	1604

Bowling: Adcock, Procter, Sinclair, Faulkner, Tayfield
Omitted with regret: Mitchell, Christy, Waite, Mann, Rowan, Lindsay, Quinn, Goddard.

The relevant fact to me on the eve of South Africa's first participation in the World Cup was that nobody in the South African squad was of sufficient ability to be chosen for the all-time team.

Measured against several of the other countries whose current teams included all-time greats – Pakistan, India, New Zealand and England – this suggested South Africa might be short on brilliance. But this was not necessarily so, and even if it were such a lack could be outweighed by strength of teamwork. A lot would depend on how this South African team blended. The probable batting line-up of the squad was:

Wessels
    Hudson
    Kirsten
    Kuiper
    Cronje
    Rhodes
    McMillan
    Richardson
    Snell
    Pringle
    Donald

Kepler Wessels, of course, was a known quantity internationally, having played for Australia during his own years of exile. A fine and dependable left-handed opening batsman, he was capable of long innings and protracted concentration and would make an experienced captain.

What interested me even more was that he was one of four Afrikaans-speakers in the team – that is persons whose first language or home language was Afrikaans – and that was a good sign of the game's growth in popularity among Afrikaners. The other three were Cronje, Tertius Bosch and, in spite of his Scottish name, Allan Donald.

In the old days cricket was so dominated by "English" South Africans that jokes were made about it. Indeed, in one of his own rare forays into humour, Prime Minister

Vorster was credited with one of the best wisecracks on the subject. When he had been busy in Parliament during debates, if there was a Test Match on, Vorster used to arrange for his secretary to come in and whisper the score in his ear from time to time. During the last England tour his secretary had whispered: "Die Engelse het vier paaltjies vir ongeveer twee honderd lopies verloor." ("The English have lost four wickets for about two hundred runs") Vorster had replied: "Hulle Engelse of ons Engelse?" ("Their English or our English?")

Andrew Hudson, the other opening batsman from Natal, was young and untried, and his selection had been strongly criticised. In fact the whole selection of the team had been controversial in that the selectors had stunned everyone by omitting Jimmy Cook, Clive Rice and Peter Kirsten, only relenting in Kirsten's case following some very heavy run scoring from him in the domestic competition. But Rice, regarded as one of the best all-rounders in the world, was an amazing omission in view of his double value. His bowling would have been invaluable in terms of the limited-overs formula of the World Cup, especially since South Africa seemed short of containment bowlers as distinct from strike bowlers. Furthermore, Cook had scored over 3000 runs in his last county season.

Adrian Kuiper was known, at least by reputation, to be a most dynamic batsman and useful medium-paced bowler – the ideal sort of player for the one-day game. Against one of the rebel "England" XIs he had hit a century off 49 balls with eight sixes and seven fours.

Hansie Cronje, only 22 years old, was already provincial captain of Orange Free State, and a batsman of exceptional promise. Jonty Rhodes, also 22, was known mainly as a superb fielder but was showing considerable promise as an aggressive batsman. South Africa were lucky to have at numbers seven and eight two such fine batsmen as Brian McMillan and David Richardson. Neither would have been out of place at number four or five in a Test side.

The pace bowling also looked strong. Allan Donald was known through his performances in English county cricket as one of the fastest bowlers in the world. Meyrick Pringle was very quick as well, as were Snell and McMillan, so with Kuiper as the fifth seam bowler South Africa didn't look short in the pace department. For spin they had Peter Kirsten, not a full-time bowler, to supply adequate offspin, and Omar Henry, the only black member of the team, who was a left-arm spinner.

Richardson was reputed to be a wicketkeeper of the highest class, so it seemed obvious that South Africa was continuing its tradition of top-grade wicketkeeper-batsmen in succession to Cameron, Sherwell, Wade, Fullerton, Waite, Endean and Lindsay. Jennings I hadn't seen, as he had come to the fore during my years of exile, but there were those observers who ranked him as high as any of the others as a gifted wicketkeeper.

My only negative thought about the South African team was that while it, like the strong Pakistan team, looked potentially a powerful five-day Test Match side with its battery of strike bowlers, it seemed short of the containment specialists who were doing so well in the one-day game – the Pringle, Reeve, De Freitas types who were able to close up an end and so choke up the supply of runs, that frustration set in resulting either in wickets or in inadequate run-rates.

A Trevor Goddard, bowling his nagging left-arm medium-pacers at middle and leg, would have been the perfect one-day player, especially with his marvellous batting and fielding as well. Then there were all those batsmen inexperienced at the highest international level. It was true that they had played international players in the rebel teams, but never full teams of Test Match players of the first rank. Could the young batsmen adjust to the different tempo challenges of the World Cup formula?

We would soon see! The aircraft was sweeping in over the ocean to land at Sydney! I put away all my charts and books and statistics, all my memories and estimates and theories. From now on there would be facts to go on – actual matches, innings, bowling spells. Deeds, not imaginings!

Within a few days I would see this new South African team for myself; would see them take the field at the Sydney Cricket Ground against Australia ... But first Australia had to play New Zealand in Auckland, and England had to play India in Perth.

The World Cup was on!

PART TWO

The Matches

NEW ZEALAND v AUSTRALIA
A Good Kick up the Backside
Auckland, February 22

In this opening match of the 1992 World Cup at Eden Park, New Zealand were soon in difficulties, losing two wickets for only 13 runs as the Australians went all out to break through their top-order batting. Andrew Jones, one of the main Kiwi hopes, went for only four runs.

There was a special edge to the match between the two host countries, each determined to outperform the other as the regional winner, though in view of the early Australian breakthrough the Kiwi batting began to look fragile.

Then Martin Crowe, always a batsman of obvious class, began to assert the authority of his strokeplay. The movements of his bat, all deliberate ease and precision, reminded me at times of a right-handed David Gower in top form. Lazily he swept the ball to square leg. Indolently he drove through the covers. Again and again he pierced the field until the Australians seemed not to know what sort of field to set for him.

Rutherford stayed with Crowe who was now letting the bat go through harder and harder, without seeming to give a semblance of a chance to the bowlers.

Even the normally economical bowling of Steve Waugh was costing six runs an over as Crowe took the Kiwi total past the 200 mark, and with Rutherford run out for 57 Crowe stepped up the tempo of his attack even further to take New Zealand to the healthy total of 248 for six in the allotted 50 overs, reaching his own century exactly.

When Australia batted we saw an interesting manifestation of Crowe's imaginative captaincy. Reaching back more than 100 years to the tactics of international cricket in the nineteenth century, Crowe opened with a spinner, Dipak Patel, at one end. Patel, who bowls accurate offspin and sometimes drifts the ball out a little off a perfect length, never looked threatening as an attack bowler, but proved his worth in driving the Australian batsmen to frustration.

At the other end Crowe kept switching medium-pacers around frequently to unsettle the Australians with variety – if not class bowling. On all but David Boon these tactics worked, but Boon, whose brutal bludgeonings with the bat are in such stark contrast to the elegance of Crowe, nevertheless replied to Crowe's century by matching it exactly.

However, Boon had little support from his middle order and the Australians fell short by 37 runs, registering the first shock of the 1992 World Cup – New Zealand's win!

The Australians seemed dazed by this defeat as they flew back from Auckland, Allan Border offering the strange comment: "Once again we find ourselves with a good kick up the backside. Maybe it's the shot in the arm we need to get back into one-day cricket." Such an anatomical confusion of metaphors reminded one of the schoolboy phrase describing those so mixed-up that they didn't know their arses from their elbows.

News of Australia's defeat was flashed to the England camp in Perth, where England's match against India started on the same day but several time zones later.

NEW ZEALAND			AUSTRALIA		
RT Latham c Healy b Moody		26	DC Boon run out		100
JG Wright b McDermott		0	GR Marsh c Latham b Larsen		19
AH Jones lbw b Reid		4	DM Jones run out		21
*MD Crowe not out		100	*AR Border c Cairns b Patel		3
KR Rutherford run out		57	TM Moody c and b Latham		7
CZ Harris run out		14	ME Waugh lbw b Larsen		2
+ IIDS Smith c Healy b McDermott		14	SR Waugh c and b Larsen		38
CL Cairns not out		16	+IA Healy not out		7
			CJ McDermott run out		1
			PLTaylor c Rutherford b Watson		1
DN Patel, GR Larsen and W Watson did not bat.			BA Reid c Jones b Harris		3
Extras (lb 6, w 7, nb 4)		17	Extras (lb 6, w 2, nb 1)		9
TOTAL (6 wkts, 50 overs)		248	TOTAL (48.1 overs)		211

FALL OF WICKETS: 1-2, 2-13, 3-53, 4-171, 5-191, 6-215
BOWLING: McDermott 10-1-43-2 (w 2), Reid 10-0-39-1 (nb 4, w 2), Moody 9-1-37-1, S R Waugh 10-0-60-0 (w2), Taylor 7-0-36-0, M Waugh 4-0-27-0 (w.1)

FALL OF WICKETS: 1-62, 2-92, 3-104, 4-120, 5-125, 6-199, 7-200, 8-205, 9-206
BOWLING: Cairns 4-0-30-0 (w 1, nb 1), Patel 10-1-36-1, Watson 9-1-39-1 Larsen 10-1-30-3 Latham 8-0-35-1 Harris 7.1-0-35-1.

Umpires: Khizar Hayat (Pakistan) and DR Shepherd (England)
Man of the Match: MD Crowe
NEW ZEALAND WON BY 37 RUNS

ENGLAND V INDIA
Licensed to Kill

Perth, February 22

England began the campaign for the World Cup with their new-look opening partnership of Gooch and Botham, the first match being against tough opponents and former title holders, India. A good omen for England and a bad one for India was that Graham Gooch was dropped by the wicketkeeper, Kiran More, before he had scored. More must have had some nightmarish twinges over this, because the last time he had dropped Gooch the latter had gone on to score 333 at Lords. This time Gooch got a half-century despite an attack of cramp. Ian Botham, after being out early for nine, acted as his runner.

The star of the England innings was Robin Smith who made a brilliant 91 in 108 balls, including two huge sixes over the 80-metre mid-wicket boundary at the WACA ground. As always when he is in form, Smith punctuated his brilliant shots with a manic stare to keep his eyes focused, then frenzied running on the spot. England totalled 236, and already it could be seen that the potentially heavy-scoring England line-up would be highly effective – provided Gooch kept his nerve.

Any two of the England batsmen could, in terms of ability, pile up the runs quickly enough to reach record totals. The key to a successful positive batting policy had to lie in granting the likes of Botham, Smith, Hick and Lamb "licence to kill" the bowling – with the assurance that there would be no recriminations if they lost their wickets in the process.

When India began to bat it seemed they might fairly easily reach the England total, having batsmen of the brilliance of Tendulkar, Srikkanth, Azharuddin and Kapil Dev, but then Ian Botham showed his amazing all-round abilities yet again by holding a remarkable catch to dismiss Srikkanth, taking two wickets for only 27 runs in ten overs – including the key wicket of Tendulkar – and providing the run-out to win the game for England when Banerjee had taken India to within nine runs of victory.

How people in England could talk of dropping cricketers like Botham, and for that matter Gower, remained a mystery to cricket fans in other countries. Certainly in my book Botham and Gower would have been the first two chosen, before the other nine were even considered.

The reason why some cricket officials in England opposed cricketers like Botham and Gower was because of an inadequate understanding of Gracism – W.G. Gracism.

When W.G. was asked once the key to successful run scoring he replied: "You put the bat to the ball." W.G. was also an habitual flasher outside the off stump, as are most great batsmen. In the case of Gower, the critics enthused when he flashed outside the off stump to send the ball to the boundary. Brilliant shot, they said. When he repeated the shot unsuccessfully, which required only a millimetre of misjudgment to result in a catch, they flayed him as "irresponsible". They didn't seem to see that you couldn't have the one without the other – you couldn't have the brilliance without the flashing. Botham, too, was praised when his great flailings resulted in brilliant boundaries, and excoriated when they got him out.

It had always seemed to me the height of pettiness to measure the difference between brilliance and irresponsibility by one millimetre.

However, England were off to a good start, and in the Indian camp there were already some mutterings, which I thought justified, about the burden of their pre-tournament programme of matches in Australia.

ENGLAND		
*GA Gooch c Tendulkar b Shastri		51
IT Botham c More b Kapil Dev		9
RA Smith c Azharuddin b Prabhakar		91
GA Hick c More b Banerjee		5
NH Fairbrother c Srikkanth b Srinath		24
+AJ Stewart b Prabhakar		13
CC Lewis c Banerjee b Kapil Dev		10
DR Pringle c Srikkanth b Srinath		1
DA Reeve not out		8
PAJ deFreitas run out		1
PCR Tufnell not out		3
Extras (b 1, lb 6, w 13)		20
TOTAL (9 wkts, 214 min, 50 overs)		236

FALL OF WICKETS: 1-21, 2-121, 3-137, 4-197, 5-198, 6-214, 7-222, 8-223, 9-224
BOWLING: Kapil Dev 10-0-38-2 (w 6), Prabhakar 10-3-34-2, Srinath 9-1-47-2, Banerjee 7-0-45-1, Tendulkar 10-0-37-0 (w 1), Shastri 4-0-28-1 (w 1)

INDIA		
RJ Shastri run out		57
K Srikkanth c Botham b DeFreitas		39
*M Azharuddin c Stewart b Reeve		0
SR Tendulkar c Stewart b Botham		35
VG Kambli c Hick b Botham		3
PK Amre run out		22
Kapil Dev c De Freitas b Reeve		17
S Banerjee not out		25
+KS More run out		1
M Prabhakar b Reeve		0
J Srinath run out		11
Extras (lb 9, w 7, nb 1)		17
TOTAL (207 min, 49.2 overs)		227

FALL OF WICKETS: 1-63, 2-63, 3-126, 4-140, 5-149, 6-187, 7-194, 8-200, 9-201, 10-227
BOWLING: Pringle 10-0-53-0 (w 1), Lewis 9.2-0-36-0 (w 5, nb 1), DeFreitas 10-0-39-1, Reeve (w 1) Botham 10-0-27-2, Tufnell 4-0-25-0

Umpires : PJ McConnell (Australia) and JD Buultjens (Sri Lanka).
Man of the Match: IT Botham
ENGLAND WON BY 9 RUNS

PAKISTAN v WEST INDIES
Retired Hurt but Triumphant
Melbourne, February 23

As with the other two games I watched Pakistan's match against West Indies in Melbourne on television from my hotel room in Sydney, having resolved to follow and travel with the South African team for as long as possible.

This second day of the tournament started well for Pakistan, who achieved a solid foundation to their innings. Ramiz Raja looked a polished opener with all the shots, but possibly a trifle too perfectionist in his approach. In a way the powerful Pakistani team undermined themselves by over-establishing their innings. If they had lost some wickets early by bringing in some of their dynamic attackers sooner, they would probably have achieved a far bigger total. At the top levels these days there was little time to consolidate opening stands, and though Ramiz Raja completed a worthy century, and Javed Miandad typically produced a gem of an improvisatory innings to try to hurry the scoring rate along, it all came too late against the dynamic Caribbean line-up, which ominously contained no "careful" batsmen.

Carelessly, then, irresponsibly and foolishly or – depending on one's point of view – brilliantly, efficiently and successfully, the West Indians swung the bat from the first over and massacred the Pakistani bowling to knock off the required runs without losing any wickets. Brian Lara looked brilliant, and seemed to be doing as he wished until Wasim Akram landed a very fast ball on his right toe – prompting yet again the question of why modern batsmen wear proper protection everywhere but on their feet. Lara retired hurt and there was concern about his availability for the next match, since he was clearly a star of the new side and now established in the West Indian line-up.

He was also one of an exciting new crop of young cricketers who would undoubtedly emerge from this World Cup as stars – such as Tendulkar, Chris Lewis and some of the young Pakistani and South African players if they lived up to their rumoured promise.

Among the Pakistanis Wasim Akram looked as good as he always did, sending the ball down at real speed with his whippy left-arm action – being such a good fast bowler that one tended to forget he was a tremendous attacking batsman as well.

PAKISTAN			WEST INDIES		
Ramiz Raja not out		102	DL Haynes not out		93
Aamir Sohail c Logie b Benjamin		23	BC Lara retired hurt		88
Inzamam-ul-Haq c Hooper b Harper		27	*RB Richardson not out		20
*Javed Miandad not out		57			
Extras (b 1, lb 3, w 5, nb 2)		11	Extras (b 2, lb 8, w 7, nb 3)		20
TOTAL (2wkts 50 overs)		220	TOTAL (no wkt 46.5 overs)		221

Salim Malik, Ijaz Ahmed, +Moin Khan, Wasim Akram, Iqbal Sikander, Wasim Haider and Aqib Javed did not bat.

FALL OF WICKETS: 1-45, 2-97
BOWLING: Marshall10-1-53-0 (w 3),Ambrose 10-0-40-0 (w1 nb 2), Benjamin 10-0-49-1 (w 1), Hooper 10-0-41-0, Harper 10-0-33-1

CL Hooper, KLT Arthurton, AL Logie, RA Harper, MD Marshall, +D Williams, CEL Ambrose WKM Benjamin did not bat.
BOWLING: Wasim Akram 10-0-37-0 (w 7), Aqib Javed 8.5-0-42-0 (nb 2), Wasim Haider 8-0-42-0 (nb 1), Ijaz Ahmed 6-1-29-0, Iqbal Sikander 8-1-26-0, Aamir Sohail 6-0-35-0

Umpires: SG Randall (Australia) and ID Robinson (Zimbabwe)
Man of the Match: BC Lara
WEST INDIES WON BY 10 WICKETS

ZIMBABWE v SRI LANKA
Iron Determination
New Plymouth, February 23.

Across the Tasman Sea in New Plymouth, New Zealand, Zimbabwe delighted their supporters by going on a remarkable run-spree, reminding their opponents yet again that this team, though short of resources and national depth of reserves, had a talent for causing upsets like the defeat of Australia in 1983. The 23-year-old Andy Flower scored an aggressive 115 not out and Waller smashed an astonishing 83 off 45 balls, in the process setting a new World Cup record by reaching fifty off only 32 deliveries. Waller and Flower also set a new World Cup record partnership for the fifth wicket of 145, and Zimbabwe reached the huge total of 312.

In reply Sri Lanka were soon in trouble with four wickets down in the 33rd over for 169, at which point any rational gambler knowing nothing of cricket would have placed a large wager on a Zimbabwe victory...

Arjuna Ranatunga chose the moment to celebrate becoming the first Sri Lankan to play in 100 one-day internationals by scoring an unbeaten 88 off 62 balls, while Samarasekera hit 75 off 61 and Roshan Mahanama hit a fast 59.

At one stage Sri Lanka needed nine runs per over with 15 overs to go, but Sanath Jayasuriya hit two big sixes and two fours to kick-start the innings back on course with 32 off 23 balls.

This amazing Sri Lankan reply to the Zimbabwean run-blitz astonished all concerned, because it showed that Sri Lanka's run-scoring skills — which were already well-known — could be allied to an iron determination, which had not yet registered with the cricket public.

After this avalanche of runs from the Sri Lankan bats which enabled them to reach the huge total of 312 with four balls to spare and three wickets in hand, nobody was going to under-estimate the batting of the Sri Lankans again in this tournament.

ZIMBABWE

+A Flower not out	115
WR James c Tillekeratne b Wickremasinghe	17
AJ Pycroft c Ramanayake b Gurusinha	5
*DL Houghton c Tillekeratne b Gurusinha	10
KJ Arnott c Tillekeratne b Wickremasinghe	52
AC Waller not out	83
Extras (lb 6, b 2, w 13, nb 9)	30
TOTAL (4 wkts 50 overs)	312

KG Duers, IP Butchart, EA Brandes, MP Jarvis and AJ Traicos did not bat

FALL OF WICKETS: 1-30, 2-57, 3-82, 4-167

BOWLING: Ramanayake 10-0-59-0 (w 3, nb 1), Wijegunawardena 7-0-54-0 (w 3, nb 6) Wickremasinghe 10-1-50-2 (w 1, nb 2), Gurusinha 10-0-72-2 (w 6), Kalpage 10-0-51-0, Jayasuriya 3-0-18-0

SRI LANKA

RS Mahanama c Arnott b Brandes	59
MAR Samarasekera c Duers b Traicos	75
*PA de Silva c Houghton b Brandes	14
AP Gurusinha run out	5
A Ranatunga not out	88
ST Jayasuriya c Flower b Houghton	32
+HP Tillekeratne b Jarvis	18
RS Kalpage c Duers b Brandes	11
CPH Ramanayake not out	1
Extras (w 5, lb 5)	10
TOTAL (7 wkts 49.2 overs)	313

KIW Wijegunawardene and AGD Wickremasinghe did not bat

FALL OF WICKETS: 1-128, 2-144, 3-155, 4-167, 5-212, 6-273, 7-309

BOWLING: Jarvis 9.2-0-61-1(w 1), Brandes 10-0-70-3, Duers 10-0-72-0, Butchart 8-0-53-0 (w 3), Traicos 10-1-33-1 (w 1), Houghton 2-0-19-1

Umpires: PD Reporter (India) and SJ Woodward (New Zealand)

Man of the Match: A Flower

SRI LANKA WON BY 3 WICKETS

SRI LANKA v NEW ZEALAND
Negative Containment
Hamilton, February 25

Sri Lanka were already starting to feel the effects of an arduous itinerary. For some reason they were being required to travel more extensively and crowd in more fixtures in less time than the other national teams. In this case they were being called on to play two matches before the South Africans had even played one.

Batting first, they reached a modest 206 for nine against the steady New Zealand bowling – partly a reaction following their run-orgy against Zimbabwe and partly a natural response to the rather negative containment-above-all policy of New Zealand. In the event Sri Lanka proved over-cautious, and although Mahanama's 81 was a technically impressive innings, he used up too much crease-time.

Replying, New Zealand cruised comfortably past the 206 target, Ken Rutherford carrying his bat for 65 with support from Wright – 57, Jones – 49, and Latham – 20. It was a rather boring match between two defensive sides on the day, with no attacking bowler on either side.

Meanwhile the South African team had arrived at their Sydney hotel, together with many old friends of mine in the South African media accompanying the team, and it was good to meet and talk with them all, wishing the team luck for their momentous first game against Australia at the Sydney Cricket Ground. They seemed a bright-eyed, lively lot, and it was good to see Peter Kirsten from my home town and exchange news of mutual friends.

They were all agog over the announcement by President De Klerk that he was calling a referendum in South Africa to seek a mandate from white voters to continue his reform policies. To the cricketers, of course, the news was momentous, because presumably if the referendum were lost it would be the end of moves away from apartheid and therefore also the end of international sport and participation in the World Cup.

Most of us in the South African party felt De Klerk would win the referendum, though possibly by a narrow margin. Pressed by the Australian television and radio reporters for a figure, I guessed at 55% – though I said I would settle for 51%!

Dr Frederick Van Zyl Slabbert, former Leader of the Opposition and of the Progressive Federal Party, was visiting Sydney and also felt the vote would be won.

But there were several members of the team who were deeply concerned, nonetheless, and while they welcomed the reassurances of older politicos, you could see they would believe the good news when they saw it and not before.

SRI LANKA

RS Mahanama c and b Harris		81
MAR Samarasekera c Wright b Watson		9
AP Gurusinha c Smith b Harris		9
*P de Silva run out		31
A Ranatunga c Rutherford b Harris		20
ST Jayasuriya run out		5
+HP Tillekeratne c Crowe b Watson		8
RS Kalpage c Larsen b Harris		11
CPH Ramanayake run out		2
SD Anurasiri not out		3
GP Wickremasinghe not out		3
Extras (b 1, lb 15, w4, nb 5)		25
TOTAL (9 wkts, 50 overs)		206

FALL OF WICKETS: 1-18, 2-50, 3-120, 4-172, 5-172, 6-181, 7-195, 8-199, 9-202
BOWLING: Morrison 8-0-36-0, Watson 10-0-37-3, Larsen 10-1-29-0, Harris 10-0-43-3, Latham 3-0-13-0, Patel 9-0-32-0

NEW ZEALAND

JG Wright c and b Kalpage		57
RT Latham b Kalpage		20
AH Jones c Jayasuriya b Gurusinha		49
*MD Crowe c Ramanayake b Wickremasinghe		5
KR Rutherford not out		65
CZ Harris not out		5
Extras (lb 3, w 3, nb 3)		9
TOTAL (4 wkts 48.2 overs)		210

DN Patel, +IIDS Smith, GR Larsen, DK Morrison and W Watson did not bat
FALL OF WICKETS: 1-77,2-91,3-105,4-186
BOWLING: Ramanayake 9.2-0-46-0 (w 2), Wickremasinghe 8-1-40-1 (w 1), Anurasiri 10-1-27-0, Kalpage 10-0-33-2, Gurusinha 4-0-19-1, Ranatunga 4-0-22-0, Jayasuriya 2-0-14-0, De Silva 1-0-6-0

Umpires PD Reporter (India) DR Shepherd (England)
Man of the Match: KR Rutherford
NEW ZEALAND WON BY 6 WICKETS

AUSTRALIA v SOUTH AFRICA
Mayhem
Sydney, February 26

It was an intensely emotional moment for many, not least for me, as the first South African team to play abroad in 28 years walked out on to the Sydney Cricket Ground in their dark green uniforms to a standing ovation from the capacity crowd. They looked a big, athletic team as they practically ran to their positions almost as if they could hardly wait to pick up the torch of the Pollocks, Nourses and Taylors of the past.

The ground looked magnificent, a perfect setting for their comeback, and the atmosphere was electric with the home team under pressure to make up for their unfortunate lapse in Auckland. I was located in the press box at the top of the Noble Stand, looking directly across at what used to be the Hill and which is now covered in seating, some of it forming the multi-tiered Doug Walters Stand. There was something about this great ground that I couldn't understand – no Victor Trumper Stand! There was the O'Reilly Stand, the Noble Stand, the Bradman and the Walters – all well deserved – but for the greatest of all the sons of New South Wales there was no stand...

But that could be the only complaint in this superb stadium where amenities were such, and good food and drink so available, that I wished members of the Lord's catering staff could be flown to Sydney and shown how to function properly.

Boon and Marsh opened the batting for Australia and total silence descended on the ground as Allan Donald began his long run-up to deliver the first ball. Then – sensation! A wicket off the first ball! Donald's very fast opening delivery had swung away, taken the edge of Marsh's bat loudly and perceptibly and carried into Richardson's gloves as all the South Africans jumped triumphantly into the air. But the umpire wasn't sure, and gave Marsh not out.

I felt proud of the reaction of the South Africans, because in spite of what this wicket would have meant to them, and in view of all the pressures on them from home to do well, they accepted the verdict without any public petulance and got on with the next delivery. Allan Donald's speed drew gasps from spectators who hadn't seen him before, and from the other end Meyrick Pringle also looked very sharp, although one-day wides and no-balls proliferated in the early overs, and the South African fielders, being over-eager, fumbled the ball several times before they settled down.

During the first ten overs the South African attack looked aggressive and penetrative, but proved expensive. The speed, if anything, helped the batsmen when line and length strayed, enabling them to get around five runs per over initially. Donald's action was rapier-like. Tall and broad-shouldered, he had a classical side-on style, whipping the ball through lissomely at an impressive pace. Pringle, however, had a more obvious aggression, banging the ball down with an air of brutality and reminding one rather of Peter Heine in his dispensation with finesse.

What a difference there was between this Pringle and Derek Pringle of England!

Derek of Essex had rounded edges to his body, and in his bowling harboured no malice towards the batsman, whereas Meyrick Pringle had a kind of lean menace that set him apart, having about him something of the assassin.

There was a Clint Eastwood quality to his thin-lipped, narrow-eyed gaze at the batsman as he turned, slightly unshaven, to begin his attack, and you could almost hear the coyotes call as he ran in with destructive intent. An interesting man, Meyrick Pringle, having grown up on an Eastern Cape farm, speaking fluent Xhosa. He was now based in Cape Town, playing for Western Province with glorious Newlands as his home ground.

Just as I was expressing how impressed I was with the pace of Pringle and Donald, McMillan and Snell took over and I became even more impressed. McMillan, a Keith Miller type of all-rounder who can play the big innings, bowled in my opinion as fast as the first two through a good delivery with a very fast arm-action, and Richard Snell also worked up a fine pace at the other end. Imperceptibly we became aware as Snell and McMillan were bowling that the Australians were losing the initiative. Slightly stunned by the speed of the opening pair, they seemed shocked now to be faced with an equally hostile fast pair, and it was almost like watching a white West Indian side because of the contrasting styles of the fast bowlers.

Snell, in particular, had a quality similar to what is often observed in West Indian fast bowlers, of appearing to be pulled into the delivery zone by the left hip – generally the result of a highly flexible, whippy body action once pronounced in the young Malcolm Marshall and in the great Michael Holding in his prime. McMillan, on the other hand, was even more able than the other three fast bowlers to produce sudden bounce – as if, in one critic's words, he suddenly produced a rubber ball. This surprise ball of McMillan's would soar away sharply towards second slip from a fullish length on the stumps, and was a deadly wicket taker.

On this showing, however, Snell impressed me the most, spearing the ball in at a very sharp pace indeed and with such accuracy that I didn't count one loose ball in his remarkable spell of eight overs for twelve runs.

Boon, by now frustrated at being unable to dominate, ran himself out and the fifth pace bowler, Adrian Kuiper, suddenly struck with successive balls, getting Marsh caught behind and Border bowled. From then on Snell, Pringle, McMillan, Kuiper and Cronje took an increasingly vice-like grip on the Australians until Allan Donald returned to blow the innings away with sheer speed. He ended with three for 34 in ten overs; McMillan had two for 35 in ten and Kuiper's two wickets in five overs cost 15.

Young Jonty Rhodes of Natal showed why his remarkable fielding was said to evoke memories of the great Colin Bland. He was hyperactively everywhere and his returns to the stumps had a snap and accuracy that drew repeated applause. Ultimately the Australians could manage only 170 runs. But the question now was – could the new boys among the South African batsmen overcome their nerves and match the deeds of their bowlers at this exciting stage?

Kepler Wessels took Andrew Hudson in with him to open the batting, and this young man acted as if batting at the SCG before a capacity crowd was all in the day's work for him. Showing touches of real class he cut, drove and glanced the Australian opening attack with every evidence of enjoyment, while Wessels at the other end appeared to have a bat with a widening blade.

Hudson, on 28, then tried to hit offspinner Taylor out of the ground, or so it appeared, only to lose his wicket, but by then the foundation was laid and Wessels and Peter Kirsten knocked off the rest of the runs without fuss, South Africa beating Australia by nine wickets. Wessels ended up with 81 not out and Kirsten on 49 not out.

Without seeing the rest of what was reputed to be a long batting line-up, I was impressed with what I had seen. I had known South Africa had strike bowlers, but I'd expected them in their inexperience of the one-day game to spray the ball around without too much control. Yet after the early nervousness in Sydney they had become as tight of line and length as their were positive in their aggression, which boded well for their progress through this tournament.

There was mayhem in the South African dressing-room within moments of their victory, and at the centre of it all a black man and a white man embraced. They were Peter Kirsten, who had just helped hit the winning runs, and Steve Tshwete of the African National Congress, who with Dr Ali Bacher had led the moves towards unity between blacks and whites in cricket and had been a key figure in making this tournament possible for the South Africans.

But Tshwete's main reason for embracing Kirsten was that both come from the same home town, East London, capital of the sports province of Border (the border between the Cape Province and Natal) whose supporters routinely chant the word in urging their teams on: "Border! Border! Border!"

I had joked earlier with some other South Africans that the Australian crowd had unwittingly committed a terrible blunder. At a key stage of the match when the Australian captain, Allan Border, had come on to bowl at the Randwick end to Peter Kirsten thousands of the Australians, knowing not what dreadful forces they were unleashing, innocently began to chant: "Border! Border! Border!" Whereupon Kirsten's reflex attack on the bowling was enough to ensure the victory. There was of course awareness throughout that South African dressingroom celebration that President De Klerk would find the victory over Australia a great help in his campaign for a yes vote in his referendum...

Several time zones away in South Africa there was equal celebration going on, and through many minds passed the thought that the end of sports isolation was a heady experience, not lightly to be thrown away with a vote against the very process of reform that had ended the isolation.

AUSTRALIA
GR Marsh c Richardson b Kuiper	25
DC Boon run out	27
DM Jones c Richardson b McMillan	24
*AR Border b Kuiper	0
TM Moody lbw b Donald	10
SR Waugh c Cronje b McMillan	27
+IA Healy c McMillan b Donald	16
PL Taylor b Donald	4
CJ McDermott run out	6
MR Whitney not out	9
BA Reid not out	5
Extras (lb 2, nb 4, w 11)	17
TOTAL (9 wkts, 49 overs)	170

SOUTH AFRICA
*KC Wessels not out	81
AC Hudson b Taylor	28
PN Kirsten not out	49
Extras (b 5, nb 2, w 6)	13
TOTAL (1wkt, 46.5 overs)	171

WJ Cronje, AP Kuiper, JN Rhodes, BM McMillan, +DJ Richardson, RP Snell, MW Pringle and AA Donald did not bat.

FALL OF WICKETS: 1-42, 2-76, 3-76, 4-97, 5-108, 6-143, 7-146, 8-156, 9-161
BOWLING: Donald 10-0-34-3 (w 5), Pringle 10-0-52-0 (w 1), Snell 9-1-15-0, McMillan 10-0-35-2 (3), Kuiper 5-0-15-2 (w 1), Cronje 5-1-17-0 (w 1)

FALL OF WICKET: 1-74
BOWLING: McDermott 10-1-23-0 (nb 2), Reid 8.5-0-41-0 (w 4), Whitney 6-0-26-0, Waugh 4-1-16-0 (w 1), Taylor 10-1-32-1 (w 1), Border 4-0-13-0, Moody 4-0-15-0

Umpires: BR Aldridge (New Zealand) and SN Bucknor (West Indies)
Man of the Match: KC Wessels
SOUTH AFRICA WON BY 9 WICKETS

PAKISTAN V ZIMBABWE
Speed and Aggression
Hobart, February 27

Pakistan, presumably still somewhat bruised after the hiding from the West Indies in Melbourne, took it out on the Zimbabwean bowlers. They raced to 254 for four, an innings dominated by an almost frenzied knock by Aamir Sohail, who was dropped four times in scoring his century. As an opener Aamir was looking suitably aggressive, as if to become the ideal foil for the more methodical Ramiz Raja, and some magnificent shots heralded yet another dimension of the dangerous-looking Pakistani team. Javed Miandad, almost predictably, continued his good form with 89 off only 93 balls.

In reply Zimbabwe struggled. They couldn't handle the speed and aggression of Wasim Akram, who became the first Pakistani other than the great Imran himself to take 150 wickets in one-day internationals.

Good in patches as some of the Zimbabwe batting had been in this and the previous match, the bowling had still looked rather weak, and the Pakistani batsmen certainly made hay while the sun shone. But Brandes the paceman was capable of bowling better and we knew too the ability of the oldest man in the tournament, John Traicos, the Zimbabwean offspinner, who had played Test cricket for South Africa in his early twenties and was now 45.

PAKISTAN		ZIMBABWE	
Ramiz Raja c Flower b Jarvis	9	KJ Arnott c Wasim b Iqbal	7
Aamir Sohail c Pycroft b Butchart	114	+A Flower c Inzamam b Wasim	6
Inzamam-ul-Haq c Brandes b Butchart	14	AJ Pycroft b Wasim	0
Javed Miandad lbw b Butchart	89	*DL Houghton c Ramiz b Aamir	44
Salim Malik not out	14	A Shah b Aamir	33
Wasim Akram not out	1	A Waller b Wasim	44
		IP Butchart c Miandad b Aqib	33
		EA Brandes not out	2
		AJ Traicos not out	8
Extras (lb 9, nb 4)	13	Extras (b3, lb 15, w 6)	24
TOTAL (4 wkts 50 overs)	254	TOTAL (7 wkts, 50 overs)	201

*Imran Khan, +Moin Khan, Aqib Javed, Mushtaq Ahmed and Iqbal Sikander did not bat.
FALL OF WICKETS: 1-29, 2-63, 3-208, 4-253
BOWLING: Brandes 10-1-49-0 (nb 4), Jarvis 10-1-52-1, Shah 10-1-24-0, Butchart 10-0-57-3, Traicos 10-0-63-0

WR James and MP Jarvis did not bat.
FALL OF WICKETS: 1-14, 2-14,3 -33, 4-103, 5-108, 6-187, 7-190
BOWLING: Wasim 10-2-21-3 (w 3), Aqib 10-1-49-1 (w 1), Iqbal 10-1-35-1 (w 1), Mushtaq 10-1-34-0, Aamir 6-1-26-2, Salim 4-0-18-0 (w 1)

Umpires: SG Randall (Australia) and JD Buultjens (Sri Lanka)
Man of the Match: Aamir Sohail
PAKISTAN WON BY 53 RUNS

WEST INDIES v ENGLAND
Handcuffs and Shackles
Melbourne, February 27

The West Indies batted first in the great stadium in Melbourne and it was a revelation to see how ruthlessly the Englishmen went about shackling the West Indian batsmen, then handcuffing them and ultimately suffocating them through sheer containment.

It was fascinating to see the different approaches of the various teams to the goal of winning the World Cup. Pakistan, like the West Indies, seemed to be going for wickets through their strike bowlers, whereas England and New Zealand were increasingly perfecting the system of containment and frustration through accuracy and non-pace.

Neither the Englishmen nor the New Zealanders were giving opposing batsmen much pace to use. The batsmen were having to generate their own pace on the ball, and this was driving the West Indians, in particular, to distraction. As men who loved the ball to come on to the bat, they were having to adjust their timing sometimes in midstroke – not a good idea generally in international cricket of any kind.

Derek Pringle opened the bowling – an interesting new ploy of Gooch's – and bowled seven overs for 16 runs, which was downright maddening to the Caribbean dynamos. Then just when they thought they were rid of the niggling Pringle along came Chris Lewis to take three wickets for 30 runs in eight overs, De Freitas with three for 34 in nine overs, Botham with one wicket for 30 in ten overs and Reeve one for 23 in ten overs.

Nothing could have been better designed to render the West Indians mute with frustration, and as I watched the line and length the Englishmen were maintaining against some of the most gifted attacking batsmen in the world I realised anew what a very good side this England team were in this World Cup format.

When England batted Gooch and Botham put up the half-century without loss, by which time the back of the West Indian attack was broken, and when Botham went out Hick casually knocked up 54 not out to go with Gooch's 65 not out, attaining victory by nine wickets with consummate ease.

At this rate it was hard to see who would keep the title from England in the final, but I had high hopes for an England-South Africa final, and who knew what the boys from the veld could yet do?

WEST INDIES

DL Haynes c Fairbrother b De Freitas		38
BC Lara c Stewart b Lewis		0
*RB Richardson c Botham b Lewis		5
CL Hooper c Reeve b Botham		5
KLT Arthurton c Fairbrother b DeFreitas		54
AL Logie run out		20
RA Harper c Hick b Reeve		3
MD Marshall run out		3
+D Williams c Pringle b De Freitas		6
CEL Ambrose c De Freitas b Lewis		4
WKM Benjamin not out		11
Extras (lb 4, w 3, nb 1)		8
TOTAL (207 mins, 49.2 overs)		157

ENGLAND

*GA Gooch st Williams b Hooper		65
IT Botham c Williams b Benjamin		8
RA Smith c Logie b Benjamin		8
GA Hick c and b Harper		54
NH Fairbrother not out		13
+AJ Stewart not out		0
Extras (lb 7, w 4, nb 1)		12
TOTAL (4 wkts, 39.5 overs, 164 mins)		160

DA Reeve, CC Lewis, DR Pringle, PAJ De Freitas and PCR Tufnell did not bat.

FALL OF WICKETS: 1-0, 2-22, 3-36, 4-55, -91, 6-102, 7-116, 8-131, 9-145, 10-157
BOWLING: Pringle 7-3-16-0, Lewis 8.2-1-30-3 (nb 1), De Freitas 9-2-34-3 (w 2), Botham 10-0-30-1, Reeve 10-1-23-1 (w 1), Tufnell 5-0-20-0.

FALL OF WICKETS: 1-50, 2-71, 3-126, 4-156
BOWLING: Ambrose 8-1-26-0, Marshall 8-0-37-0 (nb 1, w 2), Benjamin 9.5-2-22-2 (nb 1, w 2), Hooper 10-1-38-1, Harper 4-0-30-1

Umpires: KE Liebenberg (South Africa) and SJ Woodward (New Zealand)
Man of the Match: CC Lewis
ENGLAND WON BY 6 WICKETS

INDIA v SRI LANKA
A Washout
Mackay, February 28

This match was washed out after only two balls, each side getting one point.

Already the rain rules of this tournament were becoming the subject of heated debate, along with the notion of staging a match so deep into the tropics at this season of the year. Both the Indians and the Sri Lankans felt aggrieved, and justifiably, in my opinion, at having to travel to such remote areas where the other teams were not required to do so.

The regulations agreed on in Australia for games shortened by rain were sounding increasingly bizarre, and captains were heard practically praying that they would not be on the wrong side of a rain-delay decision.

It seemed, according to the system, that the rain-delay rule massively favoured the team batting longest, in that the heaviest-scoring overs were taken by the umpires in setting the target for the other team.

It also seemed, after several expositions of this rule, that it was well-nigh impossible to understand...

By this time I had travelled with the South African team to Auckland in readiness for their match against New Zealand, and when the plane landed at Auckland airport I found the press waiting for me, because in 1981 I had been brought to New Zealand by HART (Halt All Racist Tours) to help stop the South African rugby tour to New Zealand of that year. The young New Zealanders of HART had succeeded in that campaign after weeks of bitter demonstrations, public violence stemming from the Muldoon government's aggressive police actions against the demonstrators. Amid nationwide uproar the rugby tour had been aborted.

The New Zealand press were interested, in view of that past, to see me travelling with and supporting the tour of the 1992 South African team. I explained that as the apartheid laws had been repealed, and because no less a person than Nelson Mandela had given his and the ANC's blessing to this tour, I was for it as well. I quoted them Steve Biko's saying: "If you want to help the victims of oppression, ask those victims how to help, and be guided by them."

In other words if black South Africans, the victims of apartheid, were big enough to forget the past and build for the future, by what right did white non-victims decide they were wrong and should be ignored?

I met some of my old friends in HART, some of whom still wanted to protest on the basis that it was "too early" to ease up on the sports boycott, but again I told them I believed that was a decision of black South Africans, like Steve Tshwete who was travelling with the team as I was.

In the event there were no protests, for which I was glad, because on the basis of my conversations with the South African cricketers and their manager, Alan Jordaan, they were solidly committed to a non-racial future in South Africa and to the reform process aimed at a non-racial democratic system.

I was impressed with the judgment of Kepler Wessels in one incident at Auckland airport. The photographers wanted a picture of Kepler and me, to which we both agreed, but just before the picture was taken one of the white South African supporters rushed forward with the South African flag – the "whites'" flag, the orange, white and blue one – and to my relief Kepler immediately held his hand up: "No flags, please!" It had averted an awkward moment.

INDIA		SRI LANKA
K Srikkanth not out	1	
Kapil Dev not out	0	
TOTAL (0 wkt, 0.2 overs)	1	

*M Azharuddin, A Jadeja, VG Kambli, SR Tendulkar, M Prabhakar, PK Amre, +KS More, J Srinath, S Banerjee did not bat.
BOWLING: Ramanayake 0.2-0-1-0

RS Mahanama, UC Hathurusinghe, AP Gurusinha, *PA de Silva, A Ranatunga, ST Jayasuriya, +HP Tillekeratne, RS Kalpage, CPH Ramanayake, KIW Wijegunawardene AGD Wickremasinghe.

Umpires: DR Shepherd (England) and ID Robinson (Zimbabwe)
NO RESULT

SOUTH AFRICA v NEW ZEALAND
Not Cricket?

Auckland, February 29

I
t was sunny at Eden Park as Kepler Wessels and Andrew Hudson came out to open the South African innings, and there was a big crowd. I found it a strange venue for cricket, with the pitch at a diagonal running from corner to corner and the square boundaries ludicrously close.

Within three overs the signs were not good for South Africa. The pitch was very slow, the Kiwi bowling was accurate and utterly paceless and the fielding was so good that it verged on the brilliant. Dipak Patel and Watson bowled with pinpoint accuracy, and fairly soon both Wessels and Hudson were frustrated out – respectively caught and bowled while trying to force the pace. Peter Kirsten came in and, considering that he had so little experience of such deadly slow wickets, began to play an innings of rare quality. Combining prudence with attack as he came to terms with the lifeless nature of the pitch, Kirsten hit up 90 off 129 balls, and looked as if he could have gone on to a double century or more given the time or circumstance.

It was while watching this valuable innings from the 36-year-old veteran that I remembered his father, Noel Kirsten, bringing little Peter to the Buffalo Club nets in East London, Cape Province, where we lordly grown-ups would let the youngster bowl to us and occasionally take a turn with the bat. It is a sobering thought to be that much older than a veteran cricketer...

The only South African batsmen to supply support were Richardson, who stayed for 28 runs off 53 balls, and McMillan, who ended up with 33 not out off 40 balls. McMillan looked a good batsman. His penchant for the drive, coupled with his fast bowling and general appearance reminded me again of Keith Miller. Kuiper lost his wicket in curious fashion. Caught behind off a no-ball, he had neither seen nor heard the call from square leg, and while he walked from the pitch under the mistaken impression that he was out the New Zealanders took advantage of this misapprehension to run him out.

This certainly was not cricket, and the umpires should not have given him out. As with judges, umpires have wide discretion to decide what is right or wrong, and the most important consideration should be simple fair play rather than the letter of the rules and regulations. I thought the New Zealanders must have been pretty desperate to win to resort to such unfairness, but on the other hand they had little enough in the way of talent or bowling to get wickets so perhaps one couldn't be too harsh on them.

Defending their inadequate total of 190, the South African bowlers were soon shocked by the comatose qualities of the pitch, on which speed actually assisted the batting side. They were also shocked by the brutal assault of Mark Greatbatch, who from the first ball launched a frenzied attack that bore no relation to the usual behaviour of opening batsmen.

Greatbatch does not look like an athlete. He looks like a slightly overweight Rotarian who indulges in too many business luncheons. Yet with a bat in his hand he becomes a sort of killer of the ball, and one of his three sixes in this innings went on to the roof of the north stand – a prodigious blow. He and Latham posted a World Cup record first wicket stand of 114 in 80 minutes, and Greatbatch ended up with 68 off 60 balls, getting good support from Latham (60 off 69) and Jones (34 not out). Ultimately the Kiwis needed only 34.3 overs to win the match.

Understandably, the South Africans were shell-shocked. On paper they were a far more talented side, yet even their best bowlers were savaged on the lifeless track. Apart from Kirsten, who took one wicket for 22 in seven overs with his off-spin, all the South African bowlers were severely mauled, and even Snell, who had been the most accurate bowler in Sydney, went for eight runs an over.

After the triumph of Sydney this match was a salutary lesson to the South Africans, and certain remarks were heard echoing an old Afrikaans proverb: "Van die Os op die Esel" ("From the Ox to the Donkey")

It was also noticed in passing that the New Zealanders were as cavalier with the "i" sound as the people of Natal, saying, like the Natalians, :"I hut hum wuth a fush" instead of "I hit him with a fish" or, as the Australians would say: "I heet heem weeth a feesh". Oh, well, as George Bernard Shaw said, we are divided by a common language...

The Greatbatch assault left lasting wounds, especially because not since the days of the stooped, bespectacled Clive Lloyd has a dynamic batsman looked less physically fitted to his talent.

SOUTH AFRICA	
*KC Wessels c Smith b Watson	3
AC Hudson b Patel	1
PN Kirsten c Cairns b Watson	90
WJ Cronje c Cairns b Harris	7
+DJ Richardson c Larsen b Cairns	28
AP Kuiper run out	2
JN Rhodes c Crowe b Cairns	6
BM McMillan not out	33
RP Snell not out	11
Extras (lb 8, nb 1)	9
TOTAL (7 wkts 50 overs)	190

T Bosch and AA Donald did not bat.

FALL OF WICKETS: 1-8, 2 -10, 3-29, 4-108, 5-111, 6-121, 7-162
BOWLING: Watson 10-2-30-2, Patel 10-1-28-1, Larsen 10-1-29-0, Harris 10-2-33-1, Latham 2-0-19-0, Cairns 8-0-43-2 (nb 1)

NEW ZEALAND	
MJ Greatbatch b Kirsten	68
RT Latham c Wessels b Snell	60
AH Jones not out	34
+IIDS Smith c Kirsten b Donald	19
*MD Crowe not out	3
Extras(b 1, w 5, nb 1)	7
TOTAL (3 wkts, 43.3 overs)	191

KR Rutherford, CZ Harris, DN Patel, CL Cairns, G Larsen and W Watson did not bat.
FALL OF WICKETS: 1-114, 2-155, 3-179
BOWLING: Donald 10-0-38-1 (nb 1, w 1), McMillan 5-1-23-0, Snell 7-0-56-1, Bosch 2.3-0-19-0, Cronje 2-0-14-0 (w 1), Kuiper 1-0-18-0, Kirsten 7-1-22-1

Umpires: Khizar Hayat (Pakistan) and PD Reporter (India)
Man of the Match: MJ Greatbatch
NEW ZEALAND WON BY 7 WICKETS

WEST INDIES v ZIMBABWE
A One-sided Game
Brisbane, February 29

On the same day, but some time zones later, West Indies batted first against Zimbabwe in Brisbane and surged to 220 for two, thanks mainly to Brian Lara, 72, Carl Hooper, 63, and Richie Richardson, 56, before slumping to 264 for eight. It did seem, however, that many teams would like to "slump to 264 for eight" in a one-day international.

When Zimbabwe batted they found the West Indian pace attack overwhelming, losing Andy Flower to Patterson for six, then Pycroft to Benjamin for 10. After 10 overs Zimbabwe were on 33, and after 23 overs they had only 62. All-rounder Ali Shah hit top score of 60 not out for Zimbabwe, but there was too much leeway to make up and the final Zimbabwean total was 189 for seven.

It was the third Zimbabwean defeat in three matches, although there was a general feeling that they should have won their match against Sri Lanka. World Cup attention, following this rather one-sided game, was beginning to focus now on Australia's next game, against India, at the Gabba in Brisbane.

WEST INDIES			ZIMBABWE		
PJ Simmons b Brandes		21	KJ Arnott retired hurt		16
BC Lara c Houghton b Ali Shah		72	+A Flower b Patterson		6
*RB Richardson c Brandes b Jarvis		56	AJ Pycroft c Williams b Benjamin		10
CL Hooper c Pycroft b Traicos		63	*D Houghton c Patterson B Hooper		55
KLT Arthurton b Duers		26	A Waller c Simmons b Benjamin		0
AL Logie run out		5	AD Campbell c Richardson b Hooper		1
MD Marshall c Houghton b Brandes		2	AH Shah not out		60
+D Williams not out		8	EA Brandes c and b Benjamin		6
WKM Benjamin b Brandes		1	AJ Traicos run out		8
			MP Jarvis not out		5
Extras (b 1, lb 6, nb 1, w 2)		10	Extras (lb 9, w 5, nb 8)		22
TOTAL(8 wkts 50 overs)		264	TOTAL (7 wkts 50 overs)		189

AC Cummins and BP Patterson did not bat.
FALL OF WICKETS: 1-78, 2-103, 3-220, 4-221, 5-239, 6-254, 7-255, 8-264
BOWLING: Brandes 10-1-45-3 (w 2, nb 1), Jarvis 10-1-71-1, Duers 10-0-52-1, Ali Shah 10-2-39-1, Traicos 10-0-50-1.

KG Duers did not bat.
FALL OF WICKETS: 1-24, 2-43, 3-48, 4-64, 5-132, 6-161, 7-181
BOWLING: Patterson 10-0-25-1(w 1), Marshall 6-0-23-0 (nb 2), Benjamin 10-2-27-3 (w 3, nb 3), Cummins 10-0-33-0.(w 1, nb 3), Hooper10-0-47-2, Arthurton 4-0-25-0

Umpires: KE Liebenberg (South Africa) and SJ Woodward (New Zealand)
Man of the Match: BC Lara
WEST INDIES WON BY 75 RUNS

AUSTRALIA v INDIA
A Desperate Throw
Brisbane, March 1

This match developed into the closest of the tournament so far, the result being in doubt until the last ball. The Australians batted first, and despite the early loss of two wickets were able to set a good target for the Indians, Dean Jones topscoring with 90 and David Boon, 43, and Steve Waugh, 29, contributing.

Set 236 to win after three overs of their innings were lost through rain, the Indians made a spirited response. Their captain Azharuddin hit a scorching 93 in an innings ended only through a desperate throw at the wicket by Border for a dramatic run-out. Sanjay Manjrekar was next highest with 47, and it seemed a tie would be fitting.

What happened, though, in the last tense moments was that Srinath lofted the final delivery of the match from Tom Moody for what seemed at first a winning six, but the ball dropped inside the boundary at deep mid-on – into the hands of Steve Waugh for what seemed the winning catch. But the ball popped out of Waugh's hands, apparently enabling the Indian batsmen to run the three runs they needed for victory. But Waugh, recovering quickly from dropping the catch, snatched up the ball and hurled it in to beat Raju's despairing dive. So Australia won by one run, getting their first tournament points.

AUSTRALIA		INDIA	
MA Taylor c More b Kapil	13	RJ Shastri c Waugh b Moody	25
GR Marsh b Kapil	8	K Srikkanth b McDermott	0
+DC Boon c Shastri b Raju	43	*M Azharuddin run out	93
DM Jones c and b Prabhakar	90	SR Tendulkar c Waugh b Moody	11
SR Waugh b Srinath	29	Kapil Dev lbw b Waugh	21
TM Moody b Prabhakar	25	SV Manjrekar run out	47
*AR Border c Jadeja b Kapil	10	AD Jadeja b Hughes	1
CJ McDermott c Jadeja b Prabhakar	2	+KS More b Moody	14
PL Taylor run out	1	J Srinath not out	8
MG Hughes not out	0	M Prabhakar run out	1
		SLV Raju run out	0
Extras (lb 7, w 5, nb 4)	16	Extras (lb 8, w 5)	13
TOTAL(9 wkts 50 overs)	237	TOTAL (47 overs)	234

MR Whitney did not bat.
FALL OF WICKETS: 1-18, 2-31, 3-102, 4-156, 5-198, 6-230, 7-235, 8-236, 9-237
BOWLING: Kapil 10-2-41-3 (w 1, nb 3), Prabhakar 10-0-41-3 (w 2 nb 1), Srinath 8-0-48-1 (w 1), Tendulkar 5-0-29-0 (w 1), Raju 10-0-37-1, Jadeja 7-0-34-0

FALL OF WICKETS: 1-6, 2-53, 3-86, 4-128, 5-194, 6-199, 7-216, 8-231, 9-234
BOWLING: McDermott 9-1-35-1 (w 1), Whitney 10-2-36-0 (w 3), Hughes 9-1-49-1, Moody 9-0-56-3, Waugh 10-0-50-1 (w 1)

Umpires: BR Aldridge (New Zealand) and ID Robinson (Zimbabwe)
Man of the Match: DM Jones
AUSTRALIAN WON BY 1 RUN (under Rain Rules)

PAKISTAN V ENGLAND
Strange Laws
Adelaide, March 1

Rain robbed England of almost certain victory in a controversial result to a rain-marred game. First England dismissed Pakistan for the second-lowest score in World Cup history, 74 runs. All the England bowlers picked up cheap wickets and England, batting, had made 17 for one from six overs when rain intervened.

Three hours later when play resumed only two more overs were possible before the rain pounded down and the match was abandoned with England at 24 for one. Under the rules of the tournament each side gained one point, no provision having been made for replays of rain-ruined matches. It was yet another example of the strange laws governing rain delay. In this match, if another seven overs had somehow been bowled, England would have been declared the winners and would have received two clear points, with none for Pakistan.

PAKISTAN		ENGLAND	
Ramiz Raja c Reeve b DeFreitas	1	*GA Gooch c Moin b Wasim Akram	3
Aamir Sohail c and b Pringle	9	IT Botham not out	6
Inzamam-Ul-Haq c Stewart b DeFreitas	0	RA Smith not out	5
Javed Miandad b Pringle	3		
Salim Malik c Reeve b Botham	17		
Ijaz Ahmed c Stewart b Small	0		
Wasim Akram b Botham	1		
+Moin Khan c Hick b Small	2		
Wasim Haider c Stewart b Reeve	13		
Mushtaq Ahmed c Reeve b Pringle	17		
Aqib Javed not out	1		
Extras (lb 1, w 8, nb 1)	10	Extras(b 1, lb 3, w 5, nb 1)	10
TOTAL(40.2 overs, 164 min)	74	TOTAL (1 wkt 8 overs, 42 min)	24

GA Hick, NH Fairbrother, +AJ Stewart, DA Reeve, CC Lewis, DR Pringle, PAJ DeFreitas and GC Small did not bat.

FALL OF WICKETS: 1-5, 2-5, 3-14, 4-20, 5-23, 6-35, 7-42, 8-47, 9-62, 10-74

FALL OF WICKETS: 1-14

BOWLING: Pringle 8.2-5-8-3 (nb 1), DeFreitas7-1-22-2 (w 7), Small 10-1-29-2 (w 1), Botham 10-4-12-2, Reeve 5-3-2-1

BOWLING: Aqib 3-1-7-0 (w 3, nb 1) Wasim Akram 3-0-7-1 (w 3), Wasim Haider 1-0-1-0, Ijaz 1-0-5-0

Umpires: PM McConnell (Australia) and SN Bucknor (West Indies)
MATCH ABANDONED

SOUTH AFRICA v SRI LANKA

An Anaesthetic Pitch

Wellington, March 2

Wellington, national capital of New Zealand, seemed one of the most attractive cities imaginable when the wind wasn't blowing, and its main cricket ground, the Basin Reserve, nestled attractively among the high suburban hills above the Cook Strait. But appearances were deceptive, because beneath all the loveliness of the green grass of Wellington lay death – death to pace, death to movement, death to all swift-moving spheres. As in Auckland the pitch was anaesthetic, making accurate medium to slow bowling almost impossible to score from while taking the sting out of truly fast bowling.

I took my place in the press box only to retreat from there within five minutes. Having no head for heights, I found it one of the scariest places I had ever been in. Reached via a kind of catwalk, it was located high in the roof of the main stand, suspended out over the edge of the field, and was apparently secured like a jet engine, with a movable joint, because with every current of wind the whole structure moved perceptibly. It was the combination of the height and the movement that drove me out of there, and it was a lucky circumstance because as I entered the downstairs clubroom I saw my old hero Roy McLean, now in his sixties but still looking as if he could belt sixes over the pavilion.

We had a most enjoyable chat, Roy travelling around following the team with a group organised by Neil Adcock, now based in Sydney. I had had a pleasant evening with Neil in Auckland, after seeing him with Mike Procter and noting to myself that here were the two fast bowlers in my all-time South African X1 drinking beer together.

Kepler Wessels, conscious of the slowness of the Wellington wicket, took the ultra-aggressive Adrian Kuiper out with him to open the batting. Yet try as they might the South Africans couldn't get away to a quick start. The Sri Lankan bowlers were deadly accurate and Ramanayake, in particular, bowled nine overs for only 19 runs.

Kuiper perished trying to force the pace and Kirsten, replacing him, applied his own more discreet brand of aggression, which included a sweetly-timed six back over the bowler's head. But even Kirsten could manage only 47 in 82 balls before failing in an attempt to loft another six – Hathurusinghe holding a fine catch on the boundary fence.

Once Wessels had gone for 40 runs off 94 balls without managing a single boundary the pressure on the incoming batsmen was huge, and the only two who made any further impression on the innings were McMillan, with 18 not out off 22 balls, and Jonty Rhodes. Rhodes hit the ball very hard indeed to the tune of 28 off 21 balls before falling to a catch of rare brilliance. He had smashed the ball with tremendous force to clear close mid-off Jayasuriya, but the latter, leaping up at that precise moment, pulled off a wonder catch that won applause from supporters of both teams.

An unusual feature of the match was that on the perimeter one of the advertising boards exhorted South Africans to vote yes on referendum day! An enterprising Johannesburg businessman, realising that multitudes of South Africans would see the sign on television, had rented the space...

When Sri Lanka went in to bat South Africa looked to have an uphill task, because logically a total of 195 was never enough against the talented batting of Sri Lanka, especially on a dead wicket on which fast bowlers if anything tended to help batsmen to score. Yet a burst of brilliant fast bowling by Allan Donald soon had the Sri Lankans in disarray, because despite the slow wicket Donald managed to whip the ball through at genuine speed to claim three wickets in quick succession. Unfortunately he also bowled nine wides in the process, and these were to prove costly.

McMillan and Snell bowled impressively tightly, as did Omar Henry, the left-arm spinner brought in for his first World Cup game, and these three completed their ten overs each for 34, 33 and 31 runs respectively. In fact, the South Africans fought back so well they nearly won the game. During the last over Sri Lanka needed two runs off the last two balls when Ramanayake smashed the second-last ball to the cover boundary for a well-deserved victory. The hero of the Sri Lanka innings was Arjuna Ranatunga, whose fine innings of 64 not out really wrapped up the match.

Once again South Africa had lost a match they should have won by failing to come to terms with parsimonious bowling on slow pitches, and we prepared to journey to Christchurch in the South Island for a sort of "make-or-break" match. The fact that the pitch there was marginally quicker looked to be a mixed blessing, because the combination of fast wickets and West Indian pace bowling was not normally a prospect to be relished.

SOUTH AFRICA	
*KC Wessels c and b Ranatunga	40
AP Kuiper b Anurasiri	18
PN Kirsten c Hathurusinghe b Kalpage	47
MW Rushmere c Jayasuriya b Ranatunga	4
JN Rhodes c Jayasuriya b Wickremasinghe	28
WJ Cronje st Tillekeratne b Anurasiri	3
RP Snell b Anurasiri	9
BM McMillan not out	18
+DJ Richardson run out	0
O Henry c Kalpage b Wickremasinghe	11
AA Donald run out	3
Extras (lb 9, w 4, nb 1)	14
TOTAL (50 overs)	195

SRI LANKA	
UC Hathurusinghe c Wessels b Donald	5
RS Mahanama c Richardson b McMillan	68
AP Gurusinha lbw b Donald	0
*PA de Silva b Donald	7
+HP Tillekeratne c Rushmere b Henry	17
A Ranatunga not out	64
ST Jayasuriya st Richardson b Kirsten	3
RS Kalpage run out	5
CPH Ramanayake not out	4
Extras(b 1, lb 7, w 13, nb 4)	25
TOTAL (7wkts, 49.5 overs)	198

FALL OF WICKETS: 1-27, 2-114, 3-114, 4-128, 5-149, 6-153, 7-165, 8-165, 9-186, 10-195
BOWLING: Ramanayake 9-2-19-0 (nb 1), Wickremasinghe 7-0-32-1, Anurasiri 10-1-41-3, Kalpage 10-0-38-1, Gurusinha 8-0-30-0(w 2), Ranatunga 6-0-26-2 (w 1)

GP Wickremasinghe and SD Anurasiri did not bat.
FALL OF WICKETS: 1-11, 2-12, 3-35, 4-87, 5-154, 6-168, 7-189
BOWLING: Donald 9.5-0-42-3 (w 9), McMillan 10-2-34-1, Henry 10-0-31-1 (w 2), Snell 10-1-33-0 (w 2), Kuiper 5-0-25-0, Kirsten 5-0-25-1

Umpires: Khizar Hayat (Pakistan) and SJ Woodward (New Zealand)
Man of the Match: A. Ranatunga
SRI LANKA WON BY 3 WICKETS

NEW ZEALAND V ZIMBABWE

Elements of Farce

Napier, March 3

There were elements of farce about this match, all tied up again with the increasingly controversial rules about rain delay and no provision being made for it to be replayed.

The truth was that conditions were at no time suitable for cricket, rain squalls coming and going throughout the day, and the teams were leaving and returning to the field at regular intervals.

Play started late, with the number of overs ultimately reduced to 18, and a fascinating touch was the playing of the two national anthems. The all-white Zimbabwean team stood patriotically for the anthem: "Nkosi Sikelel' iAfrika", for so long regarded by Southern African whites as a subversive song. It reminded me of the time I had seen the England women's hockey team, which had several black players, singing "God Save the Queen" while the all-white Zimbabwean women's team had responded with "Nkosi Sikelel' iAfrika". As a white Southern African by birth, I always found the anthem moving as a reminder that not all Africans were black.

The New Zealanders, batting first, lost two quick wickets, Latham and Greatbatch, bowled by Brandes and Duers respectively, but then Jones and Crowe produced batting of exceptional brilliance in the difficult conditions, adding more than 100 runs in nine overs. Crowe's 50 came off only 31 balls, and Jones's from 56.

Because of the rules governing rain-interruptions, New Zealand's highest scoring 18 overs were taken as the basis for calculating Zimbabwe's target, and as this meant around eight runs per over the New Zealand commentators were openly scornful of Zimbabwe's chances.

I thought this rather graceless, in view of Zimbabwe's sporting readiness to play in those conditions, and had a smile to myself on noting that the New Zealand commentators went all silent when Zimbabwe smashed up 22 runs off the first two overs. But inevitably the required rate was too high to sustain and Zimbabwe, gamely playing on in the thickening rain, eventually fell short by 48 runs with seven wickets lost.

This gave New Zealand a further valuable two points, putting them clear at the head of the World Cup table at that stage with four straight wins. It seemed worth noting, however, that they hadn't once had to play on a normal-paced wicket and might come to grief if faced with such a phenomenon.

NEW ZEALAND

MJ Greatbatch b Duers	15
RT Latham b Brandes	2
AH Jones c Waller b Butchart	57
*MD Crowe not out	74
CL Cairns not out	1
Extras (b 7, lb 6)	13
TOTAL (3 wkts, 20.5 overs)	162

KR Rutherford, CZ Harris, DN Patel, IIDS Smith, GR Larsen and DK Morrison did not bat.
FALL OF WICKETS: 1-9, 2-25, 3-154
BOWLING: Brandes 5-1-28-1, Duers 6-0-17-1, Shah 4-0-34-0, Butchart 4-0-53-1, Burmester 1.5-0-17-0

ZIMBABWE

+A Flower b Larsen	30
AC Waller b Morrison	11
*DL Houghton b Larsen	10
IP Butchart c Cairns b Larsen	3
EA Brandes b Harris	6
AJ Pycroft not out	13
AD Campbell c Crowe b Harris	8
AH Shah b Harris	7
MG Burmester not out	4
Extras (lb 9, w 3, nb 1)	13
TOTAL (7 wkts, 18 overs)	105

FALL OF WICKETS: 1-22, 2-41, 3-63, 4-63, 5-75, 6-86, 7-97
AJ Traicos and KG Duers did not bat.
BOWLING: Morrison 4-0-14-1 (w 2), Cairns 2-0-27-0, Larsen 4-0-16-3, Harris 4-0-15-3 (w 1), Latham 3-0-18-0, Crowe 1-0-6-0

Umpires: JD Buultjens (Sri Lanka) and KE Liebenberg (South Africa)
Man of the Match: MD Crowe
NEW ZEALAND WON BY 48 RUNS

INDIA v PAKISTAN
A Teenage Wonder
Sydney, March 3

India batted first, reaching 216 which seemed at first inadequate against the impressive Pakistani batting line-up. Leading scorers were the teenage wonder, Sachin Tendulkar, with 54 not out, Jadeja with 46, Kapil Dev with 35 and Azharuddin with 32. I couldn't understand why Tendulkar batted so low as to be not out. Most teams with someone of that talent would have batted him higher to avoid his running out of time or partners.

In the event, however, Pakistan couldn't compete, reaching only 173 with Sohail, 62, and Javed Miandad, 40, the leading scorers. Kapil Dev, Srinath and Prabhakar picked up two wickets each.

Javed Miandad disputes with umpire Peter McConnell. This match did not break the tradition of hostility between the two great cricketing nations. The umpires did not file a critical report on the grounds that they had been unable to understand the abuse.

INDIA		PAKISTAN	
AD Jadeja c Zahid b Wasim Haider	46	Aamir Sohail c Srikkanth b Tendulkar	62
K Srikkanth c Moin b Aqib	5	Inzamam-ul-Haq lbw b Kapil Dev	2
*M Azharuddin c Moin b Mushtaq	32	Zahid Fazal c More b Prabhakar	2
VG Kambli c Inzamam b Mushtaq	24	Javed Miandad b Srinath	40
SR Tendulkar not out	54	Salim Malik c More b Prabhakar	12
SV Manjrekar b Mushtaq	0	*Imran Khan run out	0
Kapil Dev c Imran b Aqib	35	Wasim Akram st More b Raju	4
+KS More run out	4	Wasim Haider b Srinath	13
M Prabhakar not out	2	+Moin Khan c Manjrekar b Kapil Dev	12
		Mushtaq Ahmed run out	3
		Aqib Javed not out	1
Extras (lb 3, w 9, nb 2)	14	Extras (lb 6, w15, nb 1)	22
TOTAL (7 wkts 49 overs)	216	TOTAL (48.1 overs)	173

J Srinath and SLV Raju did not bat.
FALL OF WICKETS: 1-25, 2-86, 3-101, 4-147, 5-148, 6-208, 7-213
BOWLING: Wasim Akram 10-0-45-0 (w 5, nb 2), Aqib 8-2-28-2, Imran 8-0-25-0 (w 1), Wasim Haider 10-1-36-1 (w 1), Mushtaq 10-0-59-3 (w 1), Aamir 3-0-20-0 (w 1)

FALL OF WICKETS: 1-18, 2-17, 3-105, 4-127, 5-130, 6-141, 7-141, 8-161, 9-166, 10-173
BOWLING: Kapil Dev 10-0-30-2 (w 5, nb 1), Prabhakar 10-1-22-2 (w 4), Srinath 8.1-0-37-2 (w 1), Tendulkar 10-0-37-1 (w 3), Raju 10-1-41-1

Umpires: PJ McConnell (Australia) and DR Shepherd (England)
Man of the Match: SR Tendulkar
INDIA WON BY 43 RUNS

Left: *Javed Miandad mocking More's appeal for a run out.*

Below: *Imran Khan run out for 0.*

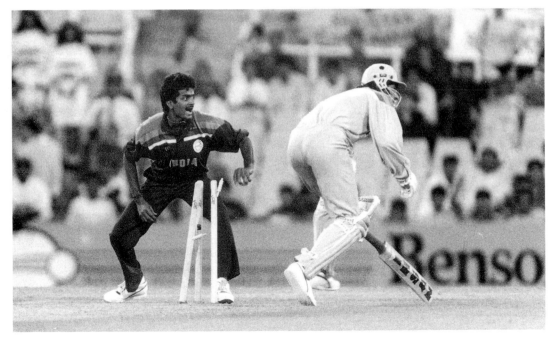

SOUTH AFRICA v WEST INDIES
An Historic Moment
Christchurch, March 5

The South African team were well aware of the importance of this "make-or-break" game, and as I watched their morning pre-match net practice it seemed to me there was a new intensity of purpose about their preparation. The sky was overcast and the outfield lush, but the bowlers reported that the pitch was better-paced than the Wellington or Auckland pitches.

West Indies won the toss and put South Africa in, and as the players took the field there was a general awareness of the significance of this historic moment – the first official match between the two countries. The extra dimension of significance was that it had long been the West Indians whose strength of boycott and depth of distaste for apartheid had led the cricket world in requiring the scrapping of apartheid laws before such a historic match could occur.

The South Africans had contemplated this confrontation with a mixture of excitement and apprehension, saying: "They're such a great team its an honour to be on the same field – but its daunting for the same reason!"

Curtly Ambrose, highest-ranking fast bowler in the world, led the West Indian attack with Malcolm Marshall, and the South African openers were soon aware of why these two great bowlers were so highly regarded. Mixing pace, aggression and accuracy they had the South Africans defending grimly, and Wessels was soon gone, caught off Marshall.

Hudson's batting impressed me enormously in this match. He played some glorious cuts from the geometric centre of the bat, which gave off mellow sounds as the ball streaked through gaps in the field. He and Kirsten had added 44 runs when he was removed through a sensational catch by Brian Lara. Rushmere, replacing him, was soon stumped off Carl Hooper, whereupon Kirsten and Kuiper responded by taking the attack to the bowlers. Kuiper at this stage struck a six so sweetly off the middle of the bat that the dreaded West Indian attack suddenly looked vulnerable.

It was, however, an illusion, and Kuiper was soon bowled by Ambrose for 23, bringing in Jonty Rhodes. Rhodes started laying about him with sharp aggression, knocking up a quick 20 before being caught behind. To their credit the South Africans kept up the attack, Kirsten again playing the dominant innings in spite of straining a leg muscle, which necessitated the assistance of a runner. Kirsten was eventually caught behind off Marshall for 56, which took him to the top of the World Cup aggregates for the tournament at this stage, with 242 runs at an average of over 80.

McMillan and Richardson, each with 20, kept the scoreboard turning over and finally, by the last allotted ball, South Africa reached 200. Against the mighty batsmen of the Caribbean it seemed far from enough – but sensational events were in prospect, deeds that could scarcely have been predicted or even hoped for by even the most optimistic South African.

Brian Lara, opening with probably the world's greatest one-day opener in Desmond Haynes, started with two brilliant boundaries off Meyrick Pringle, one being an off-drive of such superlative timing that there was scarcely any follow-through. In the words of W.G., Lara had simply "put the bat to the ball" and the ball had streaked to the boundary.

Pringle's response was to bowl like the wind, and within only a few minutes he tore the West Indian batting line-up to shreds. First he had Lara most brilliantly caught by Rhodes off a reflex shot induced by sheer speed. Then he trapped Richie Richardson lbw also through speed as well as movement off the seam, then, apparently bowling even faster, he had Hooper and Arthurton caught identically at slip by Wessels.

Clearly unused to this sort of indignity the West Indians staged a slight rally at this point, and Gus Logie and Haynes held off the fiery attack for a while. But then Snell and McMillan took over and started scorching the ball down as Donald and Pringle had done, and Haynes soon had to go off the field for treatment to his right hand, jarred several times by the shock of taking such pace. It occurred to me at this point that the West Indians, so well equipped themselves with pace bowlers for so long, had never had to face four fast men in rotation themselves as so many of their opponents had often had to. While Haynes was off the field Snell produced a hostile burst of pace to dismiss both Marshall and Williams in one over, and Haynes returned only to be caught behind off South Africa's fifth paceman, Adrian Kuiper, who for good measure got Logie three balls later. Allan Donald completed formalities soon after and the West Indies were all out – beaten by 64 runs.

SOUTH AFRICA		WEST INDIES	
*KC Wessels c Haynes b Marshall	1	DL Haynes c Richardson b Kuiper	30
AC Hudson c Lara b Cummins	22	BC Lara c Rhodes b Pringle	9
PN Kirsten c Williams b Marshall	56	*RB Richardson lbw b Pringle	1
MW Rushmere st Williams b Hooper	10	CL Hooper c Wessels b Pringle	0
AP Kuiper b Ambrose	23	KLT Arthurton c Wessels b Pringle	0
JN Rhodes c Williams b Cummins	22	AL Logie c Pringle b Kuiper	61
BM McMillan c Lara b Benjamin	20	MD Marshall c Rhodes b Snell	6
+DJ Richardson not out	20	+D Williams c Richardson b Snell	0
RP Snell c Haynes b Ambrose	3	CEL Ambrose run out	12
MW Pringle not out	5	AC Cummins c McMillan b Donald	6
		WKM Benjamin not out	1
Extras (lb 8, w 3, nb 7)	18	Extras (lb 9, w 1)	10
TOTAL (8 wkts 50 overs)	200	TOTAL (38.4 overs)	136

AA Donald did not bat.
FALL OF WICKETS: 1-8, 2-52, 3-73, 4-118, 5-127, 6-159, 7-181, 8-187
BOWLING: Ambrose 10-1-34-2 (nb 3), Marshall 10-1-26-2, Benjamin 10-0-47-1 (w 2), Cummins 10-0-40-2, Hooper 10-0-47-1 (w 1)

FALL OF WICKETS:1-10, 2-19, 3-19, 4-19, 5-70, 6-70, 7-116, 8-117, 9-132, 10-136
BOWLING: Donald 6.4-2-13-1 (w 1), Pringle 8-4-11-4 (w 4), McMillan 8-2-36-0, Snell 7-2-16-2, Kuiper 9-0-51-2

Umpires: BR Aldridge (New Zealand) and SG Randall (Australia)
Man of the Match: MW Pringle
SOUTH AFRICA WON BY 64 RUNS

AUSTRALIA v ENGLAND

Battered into Submission

Sydney, March 5

This was one of the main clashes of the tournament, and not only because of cricket rivalry. The SCG was packed for a match with an extra edge between the two old rivals – the age-old love-hate relationship between Australians and "Poms" had been exacerbated during the week following some abrasive remarks by the Australian Prime Minister, Mr Keating, in the presence of the Queen. Furthermore, according to Britain's tabloid press, the unspeakable Keating had put his loathsome arm around the Queen, almost, while introducing her to various dignitaries.

Ian Botham, never one to miss a chance to needle the Australians, made his famous remark about playing before a stadium full of descendants of convicts, or words to that effect. So battle was well and truly joined as the Australians started batting, and within a fairly short time they were going well in spite of having lost Taylor lbw to Pringle for nought and Boon run out at 35. Tom Moody and Dean Jones batted well to bring up the hundred, and Australia were starting to look well set for a big total when Chris Lewis dived to bring off a brilliant catch off to dismiss Jones. Waugh was then run out, and Moody freakishly removed when, sweeping at Tufnell, he deflected the ball first with his glove then with his boot on to the stumps.

Border began a determined recovery and was beginning to look the great batsman he is when Ian Botham suddenly produced a brilliant spell of bowling to claim four quick wickets. First he delivered a perfect outswinger which darted in at the left-handed Border, hitting the top of the middle stump, then he had Healy and McDermott caught and Taylor lbw in one of the best bowling spells he had conjured up in almost a decade.

Botham's bowling – his severity of outswing in particular – was reminiscent, in style if not pace, of the big-swerving spells he had produced in the late seventies and early eighties. He ended with the remarkable analysis of ten overs for 31 runs and four wickets, in the process becoming the top wicket-taker of the tournament to that stage, with nine victims. Then, with Australia all out for 171, Botham went in with Gooch and literally battered the Australian bowling into submission in a brilliant innings of 53 before falling to a fine diving legside catch by Healy. Gooch, 58, Smith, 30, and Hick completed England's victory by eight wickets, and this time, at least, the Poms reigned supreme.

In the course of his innings Botham had hit the ball as hard and cleanly as I had ever seen him hit it, especially past point, cover and mid-off. At times the ball seemed just a battered blur on its way to the boundary. The most remarkable all-rounder of his time – and perhaps of all time – was in full form, adorning this 1992 World Cup with his brilliance, and at this stage of the contest he was far and away the dominant personality of the tournament.

Fairbrother engulfed by the congratulations of the
England team after running out Boon.

AUSTRALIA	
TM Moody b Tufnell	51
MA Taylor lbw b Pringle	0
DC Boon run out	18
DM Jones c Lewis b DeFreitas	22
SR Waugh run out	27
*AR Border b Botham	16
+IA Healy c Fairbrother b Botham	9
PL Taylor lbw b Botham	0
CJ McDermott c DeFreitas b Botham	0
MR Whitney not out	8
BA Reid b Reeve	1
Extras (b 2, lb8, w 5 nb 4)	19
TOTAL (49 overs 208 min)	171

ENGLAND	
*GA Gooch b Waugh	58
IT Botham c Healy b Whitney	53
RA Smith not out	30
GA Hick not out	7
Extras (lb 13, w 8, nb 4)	25
TOTAL 40.5 overs 171 min)	173

NH Fairbrother, +AJ Stewart, DA Reeve, CC Lewis, DR Pringle, PAJ DeFreitas and PCR Tufnell did not bat.

FALL OF WICKETS: 1-5, 2-35, 3-106, 4-114, 5-145, 6-155, 7-155, 8-155, 9-164, 10-171
BOWLING: Pringle 9-1-24-1 (nb 3 w 1) Lewis 10-2-28-0 (w 2), DeFreitas 10-3-23-1 (w 1), Botham 10-1-31-4 (w 1) Tufnell 9-0-52-1 (nb 1) Reeve 1-0-3-1

FALL OF WICKETS: 1-107, 2-153
BOWLING: McDermott 10-1-29-0 (w 3, nb 1), Reid 7.5-0-49-0 (nb 3, w 2), Whitney 10-2-28-1 (w 1), Waugh 6-0-29-1 (w 2), Taylor 3-0-7-0 Moody 4-0-18-0

Umpires: SN Bucknor (West Indies) and Khizar Hayat (Pakistan)
Man of the Match: IT Botham
ENGLAND WON BY 8 WICKETS

Phil Tufnell the England bowler in action.

SRI LANKA v AUSTRALIA
Doing the Necessary
Adelaide, March 7

S ri Lanka batted first and soon lost Mahanama to the silliest of run-outs. The batsmen neither communicated with each other nor even looked at each other, consequently finding themselves almost at the same end and donating to Australia one of Sri Lanka's most valuable wickets for only seven runs.

After losing Gurusinha lbw to Whitney, Sri Lanka staged two mini-recoveries, both featuring the classy strokeplayer Aravinda de Silva. First with Samarasekera, 34, then with Ranatunga, 23, de Silva hit up 62, and it seemed unfair when his beautiful clean hit to the long-on boundary was intercepted short of the fence through an excellent reaching catch by Tom Moody. A man with shorter arms, Boon for instance, would not have reached the ball.

Sri Lanka totalled 189, the best of the Australian bowlers being McDermott, Whitney and Taylor, who bowled their ten overs for 28, 26 and 34 runs respectively, Taylor picking up two wickets and the others one each.

When the Australian innings began the crowd grew restless because of the extreme caution of the opening pair, Marsh and Moody, who gleaned less than 20 runs from the first ten overs.

But as their confidence grew the Australians began to hit out, and the runs were knocked off with only three wickets down – the situation being celebrated with some towering sixes.

Marsh, 60, Moody, 57, Waugh, 26, and the two not-out batsmen – Boon, on 27, and Jones, on 12, did the necessary with six overs to spare.

Yet again during this tournament I was struck by the gap between the best of the Australian batting and the low standard of the bowling, because although the bowlers had been economical against the Sri Lankans, they didn't seem able to strike with a wicket when this was most needed, as bowlers like Wasim Akram of Pakistan, Curtly Ambrose of the West Indies, and Allan Donald, Meyrick Pringle, Richard Snell and Brian McMillan of South Africa seemed able to do.

Increasingly in this tournament the Australian bowlers seemed to be seeking to emulate the pure containment approach of New Zealand, but not to be doing it as well.

And regardless of the current match, Australia somehow didn't look as if the opening pairing of Moody and Marsh was the complete answer. Marsh was still tending to get bogged down for too long.

SRI LANKA		
R S Mahanama run out		7
M A R Samarasekera c Healy b Taylor		34
A P Gurusinha lbw b Whitney		5
*PA De Silva c Moody b McDermott		62
A Ranatunga c Jones b Taylor		23
S T Jayasuriya lbw b Border		15
+H P Tillekeratne run out		5
R S Kalpage run out		14
C H P Ramanayake run out		5
S D Anurasiri not out		4
Extras (b 3, lb 6, w 5, nb 1)		15
TOTAL (9 wkts, 50 overs)		189

AUSTRALIA		
G R Marsh c Anurasiri b Kalpage		60
T M Moody c Mahanama b Wickremasinghe		57
M E Waugh c Mahanama b Wickremasinghe		26
D C Boon not out		27
D M Jones not out		12
Extras (lb 2, nb 3, w 3)		8
TOTAL (3 wkts, 44 overs)		190

G P Wickremasinghe did not bat.
FALL OF WICKETS: 1-8, 2-28, 3-72, 4-123, 5-151, 6-163, 7-166, 8-182, 9-189.
BOWLING: McDermott 10-0-28-1 (w 1), S Waugh 7-0-34-0 (w 4, nb 1), Whitney 10-3-26-1, Moody 3-0-18-0, Taylor 10-0-34-2, Border 10-0-40-1.

*A R Border, S R Waugh, +IA Healy, P L Taylor, C J McDermott and MR Whitney did not bat.
FALL OF WICKETS: 1-120, 2-130, 3-165.
BOWLING: Wickremasinghe 10-3-29-2 (nb 1, w 1), Ramanayake 9-1-44-0 (nb 2, w 2), Anurasiri 10-0-43-0, Gurusinha 6-0-20-0, Ranatunga 1-0-11-0, Kalpage 8-0-41-1

Umpires: PD Reporter (India) and ID Robinson (Zimbabwe).
Man of the Match: T M Moody.
AUSTRALIA WON BY 7 WICKETS

INDIA v ZIMBABWE
Beaten by the Weather
Hamilton, March 7

Back across the Tasman Sea, the poor Zimbabweans again had a taste of the bad New Zealand weather, their game with India being rain-shortened as their game with the Kiwis had been in Napier.

India, batting first, scored 203 for seven in 32 overs, the onslaught being led by Sachin Tendulkar with 81 from 77 balls. Under the tournament rules India's best 19 overs were totalled to set Zimbabwe a target of 158 – but the odds were against the Zimbabweans, who did well to total 104 for one after 19 overs.

The Indian bowlers raced through their 15 overs to validate the match – anything short of this would have meant an annulment of the game with one point going to each team – and with their two points assured the Indians moved into joint third place with five points from five matches.

The best of the Zimbabwe bowlers were Traicos, with three for 35, and Mark Burmester with three for 36.

INDIA		
K S Srikkanth b Burmester	32	
Kapil Dev lbw b Brandes	10	
*M Azharuddin c Flower b Burmester	12	
S R Tendulkar c Campbell b Burmester	81	
S V Manjrekar c Duers b Traicos	34	
V G Kambli b Traicos	1	
A Jadeja c Shah b Traicos	6	
+K S More not out	15	
J Srinath not out	6	
Extras (lb 3, w 3)	6	
TOTAL (7 wkts, 32 overs)	203	

ZIMBABWE		
+A Flower not out	43	
A H Shah b Tendulkar	31	
A C Waller not out	13	
Extras (b 1, lb 11, w 5)	17	
TOTAL (1 wkt, 19.1 overs)	104	

M Prabhakar and S L V Raju did not bat.

A J Pycroft, *D L Houghton, A D R Campbell, E A Brandes, I P Butchart, M G Burmester, A J Traicos and K G Duers did not bat.

FALL OF WICKETS: 1-23, 2-43, 3-69, 4-168, 5-170, 6-182, 7-184.
BOWLING: Brandes 7-0-43-1, Duers 7-0-48-0, Burmester 6-0-36-3 (w 3), Shah 6-1-38-0, Traicos 6-0-35-3.

FALL OF WICKETS: 1-79.
BOWLING: Prabhakar 3-0-14-0 (w 1), Kapil Dev 4-0-6-0 (w 2), Srinath 4-0-20-0 (w 1), Tendulkar 6-0-35-1 (w 1), Raju 2.1-0-17-0.

Umpires: JD Buultjens (Sri Lanka) and SG Randall (Australia).
Man of the Match SR.Tendulkar
INDIA WON BY 55 RUNS
(winning margin determined after rain by revised totals from highest-scoring 19 overs: India 158-4, Zimbabwe 103-1).

SOUTH AFRICA v PAKISTAN
Gravity Defied

Brisbane, March 8

On arrival in Brisbane I got in touch with a very old friend who had played in the same school cricket team at CBC Kimberley and the same Nuffield team four decades ago.

Trevor Fancutt had been one of these amazing people who could excel at any sport. As a cricketer he was a fine batsman with an elegant off-drive, and a left-arm new ball bowler who moved the ball a lot at medium pace. At rugby he was a good running flyhalf who kicked for touch with pinpoint accuracy. He had been good at athletics as well, but his real strength had been tennis.

In fact, we had been doubles partners and our two names appeared on a junior trophy through what had felt to me like false pretences, since all I had had to do was serve and get out of his way, Trevor "carrying" me right through that championship.

On leaving school he had played Davis Cup tennis and become national singles champion, and at Wimbledon he had reached the last eight in the mixed doubles with Daphne Seeney of Australia.

In the Western Province Open I had seen Trevor win the singles title by beating the current Wimbledon champion, Jaroslav Drobny, in straight sets, but he had given up tournament tennis, married Daphne Seeney, and set up a big tennis complex with her in Brisbane. One of their three sons had beaten John McEnroe at Wimbledon, and at least one of them had won the Queensland Open title, so genetics was at work.

It was good to see Trevor again and talk about the old days at school in Kimberley. He looked young for his age and supremely fit – a living advertisement for tennis!

Talking of his all-round sports skills reminded me of another remarkable case of versatility. Many years ago while working as a political correspondent in the press gallery of the South African Parliament I had been impressed, during the journalists v. M.P.s cricket match, with the leg-spin googly bowling of the elderly Member of Parliament for Constantia, Mr Hamilton Russell. And as I had heard he was a former squash champion, I began to talk to "Hammo" about the sporting achievements of his youth.

"Ah, yes, squash! Wonderful game, that!"
"Yes, but did you win championships, Hammo?"
"Yes, my boy, I was Western Province champion."
"What about other sports – did you play golf?"
"Ah, yes, golf. I loved golf."
"What was your handicap?"
"Well, scratch, actually."
"Did you enter tournaments?"
"Good heavens, yes! I used to love tournaments!"

"Did you win any, Hammo?"

"Yes, I won the Eastern Province Open and the Western Province Open. Let me see, that was in..."

"Hammo. Did you play rugby?"

"Ah, the greatest game of all! Yes, rugby! My word!"

"Did you play serious rugby, Hammo?"

"Yes, my boy! Oh, for years, especially at Oxford."

"How far did you get in rugby, Hammo?"

"I played for England, when I was at Oxford. Then when I went on to Trinity in Dublin I played for Ireland."

It was the most astonishing litany of sporting achievements, and I'd had to drag each one out of him.

After talking to Trevor Fancutt I'd felt the years roll back, including the memory of the remarkable "Hammo" Russell whose son was now Anglican Bishop of Grahamstown and the most committed white South African I knew in the cause of racial justice, having been arrested and banned.

In the film "Cry Freedom", about my friendship with Steve Biko and our family's escape from South Africa after Steve's death, there was a line of dialogue about David Russell, where Steve's wife Ntsiki was showing me through the Black Community Centre that had been set up and said: "Father Russell got this for us."

Of all Hammo's five children, all of whom had distinguished themselves professionally, he had told me he was proudest of David.

Hammo, I thought, would have been interested in the Pakistani leg-spinners if he could have been in Brisbane for the next of South Africa's challenges.

He would also have been interested politically, because he had been one of General Smuts's favourite young followers, in the developing referendum campaign back in South Africa.

The cricketers were starting to get reports of a rightwing surge for the imminent vote, but some of us in the press party tried to reassure them that this was probably a ploy to get the lazy Natal voters to the polls. Besides, we wanted the cricketers to concentrate on cricket and to beat Pakistan – a tall order!

The famous Woolloongabba Ground ("the Gabba") was a vivid scene in the bright Brisbane sunshine, and before the match started I walked around the perimeter savouring historical incidents that had occurred there. Foremost in my mind were accounts by Wally Hammond's 1946 team of how a tropical thunderstorm had so devastated the ground that the whole field had been a lake in which the stumps and bails floated about as large hailstones pounded down.

Those hailstones, it seemed, were bigger than usual, though nobody recorded the reaction of the snooty old members of the Queensland Cricket Association when Sid Barnes lifted the large block of ice from the tub used to keep the players' drinks cool, wrestled it to the fence separating the Members' Enclosure from the players' area, and tipped it over to join the other "hailstones" on the Members' lawn.

One of the grandstands at the Gabba was called the Clem Jones Stand after a former mayor of Brisbane – named for him not because he was Mayor but because he was head groundsman at the Gabba, or "Curator", as the Australians called groundsmen.

Pakistan won the toss and put South Africa in to bat, Rushmere being named to replace Kirsten, who was still suffering from the leg injury sustained against the West Indians.

Wessels was out early for seven runs but the two young players, Rushmere and Hudson, impressed with their crisp stroke-play as they went after the strong Pakistani bowling. Hudson got 54 and Rushmere 35, then Cronje and McMillan, with 47 not out and 33 respectively, took the total to 211 – Cronje's batting looking better and better as his innings progressed. Wasim Akram and Imran Khan each claimed two wickets.

When the Pakistani innings began some loose bowling gave them a flying start, but then, as had happened before, the South Africans tightened up in line and length and began to take a grip of the game.

The dynamic fielding of Jonty Rhodes was becoming a regular feature of the South African pressure on the batsmen. He was as swift as an arrow getting to the ball, and his returns to the wicketkeeper's gloves were instantaneous. In the field he was never still. Like a hyperactive Labrador retriever he kept scampering about. At the end of each over he would scamper to the umpire to retrieve the bowler's cap and sweater, then scamper to the bowler to hand these over. Then he would scamper to the next bowler, get his cap and sweater, then scamper with these to the other umpire...

Sometimes, if there was nothing to scamper for, he would scamper around anyway, occasionally running in circles around his fellow fielders just out of exuberance. Peter Kirsten said he was exhausting to field with: "Just looking at Jonty wears you out," he said.

Two wickets had fallen with the total on 50, bringing Ul-Haq and Imran in together, when the rain began to pound down from a quick build-up of rain clouds which had moved in over the ground.

It was astonishing that play resumed only an hour later. The capacity of this remarkable ground to recover from a deluge was described by Hammond back in 1946 when, to his astonishment, the lake with the floating stumps was ready for play the following day. However, extra drainage facilities have been installed since then, and we in the press box watched pools of water literally drying up before our eyes.

When play resumed the reduced-overs rule was imposed, which though it favoured South Africa seemed to me grossly undesirable. It definitely discriminated against the team batting second, in that it set them a target based on the best 36 overs of the side batting first. Pakistan therefore needed 120 more runs at a rate of eight runs per over...

Daunting as this task was, Imran Khan and Inzamam Ul-Haq set about it impressively and were actually staying within reach of the required run-rate, having added 85 runs, when they lost a wicket to the most remarkable dismissal I had ever seen on any cricket ground.

Ul-Haq had played the ball to Jonty Rhodes at point, setting off for a run, but when Imran sent him back it was a race between Ul-Haq and Rhodes. Rhodes could have thrown at the stumps, but they were side-on, and he chose to back his speed against Ul-Haq's. At this stage they were both about ten yards from the stumps, running towards them very fast. Rhodes took off in a horizontal dive moving at such speed that his entire body was parallel to the ground as his outstretched hands, holding the ball, smashed all three stumps out of the ground to run out Ul-Haq by a fraction.

The crowd, at first stunned by the extraordinary sight, exploded into prolonged applause, and as the television cameras repeatedly replayed the incident so that Rhodes's gravity-defying feat could be fully appreciated.

It turned the game, and Pakistan began losing wickets while trying to recover in order to match the ever-climbing run-rate.

Actually, even without counting Jonty Rhodes, the South African fielding was excellent, in contrast to one of the worst fielding exhibitions Pakistan could surely ever have given. In one incident the wicketkeeper hurled the ball back to the pace bowler, Aqib Javed, who wasn't looking, and it hit him in the face, knocking him out. He was taken to hospital to be checked for concussion, and was later released, pronounced shaken but recovered.

So Pakistan lost, somewhat unfairly because of the rain-delay rule, though the South Africans had looked to be on course for victory before the rain stoppage. Imran Khan must have regretted sending South Africa in to bat, when under these eccentric rules, if there was any whiff of rain in the air, it surely made sense to bat first for the optimum run-rate.

SOUTH AFRICA		PAKISTAN	
A C Hudson c Ijaz b Imran	54	Aamir Sohail b Snell	23
*K C Wessels c Moin Khan b Aqib	7	Zahid Fazal c Richardson b McMillan	11
M W Rushmere c Sohail b Mushtaq	35	Inzamam-ul-Haq run out	48
A P Kuiper c Moin Khan b Imran	5	*Imran Khan c Richardson b McMillan	34
J N Rhodes lbw b Sikander	5	Salim Malik c Donald b Kuiper	12
W J Cronje not out	47	Wasim Akram c Snell b Kuiper	9
B M McMillan b Akram	33	Ijaz Ahmed c Rhodes b Kuiper	6
+D J Richardson b Akram	5	+Moin Khan not out	5
R P Snell not out	1	Mushtaq Ahmed run out	4
		Iqbal Sikander not out	1
Extras (lb 8, w 9, nb 2)	19	Extras (lb 2, w 17, nb 1)	20
TOTAL (7 wkts, 50 overs)	211	TOTAL (8 wkts, 36 overs)	173

M W Pringle and A A Donald did not bat.
FALL OF WICKETS: 1-31, 2-98, 3-110, 4-111, 5-127, 6-198, 7-207.
BOWLING: Wasim Akram 10-0-42-2 (w 7, nb 2), Aqib Javed 7-1-36-1 (w 2), Imran Khan 10-0-34-2, Iqbal Sikander 8-0-30-1, Ijaz Ahmed 7-0-26-0, Mushtaq Ahmed 8-1-35-1.

Aqib Javed did not bat.
FALL OF WICKETS: 1-50, 2-50, 3-133, 4-134, 5-156, 6-157, 7-163, 8-170.
BOWLING: Donald 7-1-31-0 (w 7), Pringle 7-0-31-0 (w 3, nb 1), Snell 8-2-26-1 (w 1), McMillan 7-0-34-2 (w 4), Kuiper 6-0-40-3 (w 2), Cronje 1-0-9-0.

Umpires: BL Aldridge (New Zealand) and SN Bucknor (W Indies).
Man of the Match: AC Hudson.
SOUTH AFRICA WON BY 20 RUNS
(winning margin determined after rain by revised totals from highest-scoring 36 overs:
South Africa 193-5, Pakistan 173-8).

WEST INDIES V NEW ZEALAND
Salt in the Wound
Auckland, March 8

West Indies, batting first, totalled 203 with Brian Lara, 52, and Keith Arthurton, top scoring. Support was mainly from Williams, 32, Richardson, 29 and Haynes, 22. The West Indians couldn't come to terms with the notoriously slow Auckland wicket.

When New Zealand batted Mark Greatbatch started explosively as, he had against South Africa, and blasted a whirlwind 63, with Martin Crowe rubbing salt into the wound with an elegant 81 not out to hit off the runs required for the loss of only five wickets.

There was temper on the pitch between Greatbatch and Curtly Ambrose, and some elements in the Eden Park crowd started throwing bottles and other debris at third-man fieldsman Winston Benjamin. It was uncharacteristic of New Zealand behaviour, and maybe was caused by the general shock at New Zealand doing so much better than expected in the World Cup.

Only a month before they had been hammered into the ground by England; now they were on top of the tournament table with ten points from five successive wins.

WEST INDIES	
D L Haynes c and b Harris	22
B C Lara c Rutherford b Larsen	52
*R B Richardson c Smith b Watson	29
C L Hooper c Greatbatch b Patel	2
K L T Arthurton b Morrison	40
A L Logie b Harris	3
M D Marshall b Larsen	5
+D Williams not out	32
W K M Benjamin not out	2
Extras (lb 8, w 7, nb 1)	16
TOTAL (7 wkts, 50 overs)	203

NEW ZEALAND	
M J Greatbatch c Haynes b Benjamin	63
R T Latham c Williams b Cummins	14
A H Jones c Williams b Benjamin	10
*M D Crowe not out	81
K R Rutherford c Williams b Ambrose	8
C Z Harris c Williams b Cummins	7
D N Patel not out	10
Extras (lb 7, w 5, nb 1)	13
TOTAL (5 wkts, 48.3 overs)	206

C E L Ambrose and A C Cummins did not bat.

FALL OF WICKETS: 1-65, 2-95, 3-100, 4-136, 5-142, 6-156, 7-201.
BOWLING: Morrison 9-1-33-1 (nb 1, w 2), Patel 10-2-19-1 (w 1), Watson 10-2-56-1, Larsen 10-0-41-2, Harris 10-2-32-2, Latham 1-0-14-0 (w 4).

G R Larsen, +ID S Smith, D K Morrison, and W Watson did not bat.
FALL OF WICKETS: 1-67, 2-97, 3-100, 4-135, 5-174.
BOWLING: Ambrose 10-1-41-1 (w 3), Marshall 9-1-35-0 (nb 1, w 1), Cummins 10-0-53-2 (w 1), Benjamin 9.3-3-34-2, Hooper 10-0-36-0.

Umpires: KE Liebenberg (South Africa) and PJ McConnell (Australia).
Man of the Match: MD Crowe.
NEW ZEALAND WON BY 5 WICKETS

ENGLAND V SRI LANKA
Plundered Bowling
Ballarat, March 9

Batting first England plundered the Sri Lankan bowling for 280 runs for six, most of the runs coming from Fairbrother, 63, Stewart, 59, Botham, 47, and Hick, 41. This was an interesting indication of respective ability, because against the same attack the South African batsmen had been unable to break free and dominate. On the other hand, in fairness, the Ballarat wicket was considerably quicker than the Wellington one had been. Chris Lewis, after contributing 20 not out off six balls, then tore through the best of the Sri Lankan batting with four wickets for 30 runs in eight overs. For Sri Lanka Ranatunga was again top scorer with 36, but the team fell far short with 174, being beaten by 106 runs.

At close of play the English players were worried about their captain, Graham Gooch, who appeared to have a leg injury.

At this stage England and New Zealand were unquestionably the two top teams of the tournament.

ENGLAND	
*G A Gooch b Labrooy	8
I T Botham b Anurasiri	47
R A Smith run out	19
G A Hick b Ramanayake	41
N H Fairbrother c Ramanayake b Gurusinha	63
+A J Stewart c Jayasuriya b Gurusinha	59
C C Lewis not out	20
D R Pringle not out	0
Extras (b 1, lb 9, w 9, nb 4)	23
TOTAL (6 wkts, 50 overs, 213 min)	280

D A Reeve, P A J DeFreitas and R K Illingworth did not bat.
FALL OF WICKETS: 1-44, 2-80, 3-105, 4-164, 5-244, 6-268.
BOWLING: Wickremasinghe 9-0-54-0 (w 3), Ramanayake 10-0-42-1 (nb 4, w 3), Labrooy 10-1-68-1 (w 2), Anurasiri 10-1-27-1 Gurusinha 10-0-67-2 (w 1), Jayasuriya (1-0-12-0).

SRI LANKA	
R S Mahanama c Botham b Lewis	9
M A R Samarasekera c Illingworth b Lewis	23
A P Gurusinha c and b Lewis	7
*P A De Silva c Fairbrother b Lewis	7
A Ranatunga c Stewart b Botham	36
+H P Tillekeratne run out	4
S T Jayasuriya c DeFreitas b Illingworth	19
G F Labrooy c Smith b Illingworth	19
C P H Ramanayake c and b Reeve	12
S D Anurasiri lbw b Reeve	11
GP Wickremasinghe not out	6
Extras (lb 7, w 8, nb 6)	21
TOTAL (44 overs, 179 min)	174

FALL OF WICKETS: 1-33, 2-46, 3-56, 4-60, 5-91, 6-119, 7-123, 8-156, 9-158, 10-174
BOWLING: Pringle 7-1-27-0 (w 1, nb 3), Lewis 8-0-30-4 (w 2, nb 2), DeFreitas 5-1-31-0 (w 3, nb 1), Botham 10-0-33-1 (w 1), Illingworth 10-0-32-2, Reeve 4-0-14-2 (w1).

Umpires: Khizar Hayat (Pakistan) and PD Reporter (India)
Man of the Match: CC Lewis
ENGLAND WON BY 106 RUNS

Above: *Anurasiri bowling with fine economy, only twenty-seven runs coming from his full quota of overs.*

Overleaf: *Chris Lewis who won the match for England, taking 4 wickets for 30 runs in 8.*

ZIMBABWE v SOUTH AFRICA
Clash of the New Africans
Canberra, March 10

South Africa won the toss and sent Zimbabwe in, which seemed to me an unimaginatively safe approach to a game in which South Africa could have both won – and pushed up its run rate. Kepler Wessels felt, however, that two more wins would make the run-rate irrelevant in that South Africa would be in the semi-finals anyway – but there were those two wins to secure first.

Zimbabwe found it heavy going against the South African pacemen, even though the pitch was slower than most in Australia. The ground, the Manuka Oval, was most attractive; the playing area surrounded by trees and leafy walkways; the hospitality tents giving it the atmosphere of an English county ground.

Meyrick Pringle broke through early, trapping James lbw with a late-swinging ball, and thereafter there was a fairly regular fall of wickets, though several came from suicidal shots at offspinner Kirsten. Kirsten, still limping slightly, had insisted on playing in this match as batsman and bowler, and in the latter capacity he picked up three wickets, two in succession to be on a possible hat-trick at one stage.

The Zimbabweans totalled 163, McMillan, Kirsten and Cronje taking most of the wickets with three for 30, three for 31 and two for 17 respectively.

I was interested in Cronje's bowling. As in Sydney and Brisbane, he maintained reasonable accuracy, dipping the ball in quite disconcertingly from the off at medium pace, and was obviously featuring in Wessels's mind as an extra bowler in these matches.

Cronje's batting, too, interested me. Although I hadn't seen a long innings from him, I thought his batting had a kind of authority which would enable him to score big centuries in time. He looked a future captain.

During the Zimbabwean innings I had heard, from behind a hedge, two elderly, unmistakeably white South African voices, inquiring where the beer tent ("the bare tent") was to be found. On seeing the owners of the voices I was touched to observe that one wore a South African supporters' shirt, and the other a Zimbabwean supporters' shirt. Who said whites couldn't adjust to reality in Southern Africa! I also noticed two ANC flags – black, green and gold – among the rash of "white" South African flags – orange, white and blue – and thought the ANC ones looked aesthetically better.

I had put to Steve Tshwete one evening a plan to make the Springbok emblem respectable again and acceptable to blacks as well as whites. It involved the rugby authorities changing the Springbok rugby uniform slightly from green and gold jersey and white shorts, to green and gold jersey and black shorts, with the gold springbok edged in black ... A compromise worthy of Solomon?

When Wessels and Hudson went in to face the Zimbabwean attack Hudson was soon out forcing the pace, and Wessels and Kirsten repeated their Sydney partnership, adding 112 runs before Wessels was bowled swinging extravagantly – a most rare event. Kirsten ended up with 62 no out, making him top of the World Cup aggregates with 304 for thrice out, and an average of 101.33. Not bad for a veteran heading for pasture ...

Kirsten's talent with the bat was obvious in his every move, far more so than with Wessels. Yet Wessels had played two shots during his innings which bore the hallmarks of obvious class. One came when he leant forward to drive, saw in the last millisecond that the ball was a shade shorter than he had supposed, and improvised in a flash late cut of rare timing. Another was when he shaped to hook, checked, and changed stroke to a short-arm placement forward of square leg.

Late cuts are rare stokes in international cricket these days, and I noticed that Kirsten played more of them than any other batsman I had seen since Denis Compton. Like Compton, Kirsten played the late cut, in Neville Cardus's wonderful phrase, "like a schoolboy playing last-touch".

So South Africa knocked off the runs in the 46th over, advancing to third place in the tournament with eight points from four victories, lining up behind England and New Zealand for a hoped-for semi-final place.

ZIMBABWE		SOUTH AFRICA	
W R James lbw b Pringle	5	*K C Wessels b Shah	70
+A Flower c Richardson b Cronje	19	A C Hudson b Jarvis	13
A J Pycroft c Wessels b McMillan	19	P N Kirsten not out	62
*D L Houghton c Cronje b Kirsten	15	A P Kuiper c Burmester b Brandes	7
A C Waller c Cronje b Kirsten	15	J N Rhodes not out	3
A H Shah c Wessels b Kirsten	3		
E A Brandes c Richardson b McMillan	20		
M G Burmester c Kuiper b Cronje	1		
A J Traicos not out	16		
M P Jarvis c and b McMillan	17		
K G Duers b Donald	5		
Extras (lb 11, w 13, nb 5)	28	Extras (lb 4, w 2, nb 3)	9
TOTAL (48.3 overs)	163	TOTAL (3 wkts, 45.1 overs)	164

W J Cronje, B M McMillan, M W Pringle, R P Snell, +D J Richardson and A A Donald did not bat.

FALL OF WICKETS: 1-7, 2-51, 3-72, 4-80, 5-80, 6-115, 7-117, 8-123, 9-151, 10-163.
BOWLING: Donald 9.3-1-26-1 (w 1, nb 2), Pringle 9-0-25-1 (w 6, nb 3), Snell 10-3-24-0, McMillan 10-1-30-3 (w6), Cronje 5-0-17-2, Kirsten 5-0-31-3.

FALL OF WICKETS: 1-27, 2-139, 3-151.
BOWLING: Brandes 9.1-0-39-1, Jarvis 9-2-23-1, Burmester 5-0-20-0, Shah 8-2-33-1, Deurs 8-1-19-0, Traicos 6-0-26-0.

Umpires: SN Bucknor (West Indies) and DR Shepherd (England).
Man of the Match: PN Kirsten
SOUTH AFRICA WON BY SEVEN WICKETS.

INDIA V WEST INDIES
Irrelevant Rain
Wellington, March 10.

India batted first against a Caribbean pace attack which looked strange without Marshall. No reasons were advanced for his omission, though there were whispers about a slight leg-strain, or a slight lack of motivation.

Azharuddin, with 61, and Srikkanth, with 40, were the main scorers for India, Manjrekar being run out for 27. Curtly Ambrose did most of the bowling damage, not only in bowling ten overs for only 24 runs, but in getting the brilliant Tendulkar out for only four.

But shortly after India's innings the weather suddenly became a factor, and West Indians decided to go all out in case rain intervened. Brian Lara and Keith Arthurton were the main factors in winning the match, with 41 and 58 not out respectively. The fact that some rain delay meant a reduction of the West Indians' target to 195 hardly affected the issue, and the West Indians gained two more points to stand fourth in the top table behind England, New Zealand and South Africa.

INDIA	
A Jadeja c Benjamin b Simmons	27
K Srikkanth c Logie b Hooper	40
*M Azharuddin c Ambrose b Cummins	61
S R Tendulkar c Williams b Ambrose	4
S V Manjrekar run out	27
Kapil Dev c Haynes b Cummins	3
P K Amre c Hooper b Ambrose	4
+K S More c Hooper b Cummins	5
M Prabhakar c Richardson b Cummins	8
J Srinath not out	5
S L V Raju run out	1
Extras (lb 6, w 5, nb 1)	12
TOTAL (49.4 overs)	197

WEST INDIES	
D L Haynes c Manjrekar b Kapil Dev	16
B C Lara c Manjrekar b Srinath	41
P V Simmons c Tendulkar b Prabhakar	22
*R B Richardson c Srikkanth b Srinath	3
K L T Arthurton not out	58
A L Logie c More b Raju	7
C L Hooper not out	34
Extras (lb 8, w 2, nb 4)	14
TOTAL (5 wkts, 40.3 overs)	195

+D Williams, C E L Ambrose, A C Cummins, W K M Benjamin did not bat.

FALL OF WICKETS: 1-56, 2-102, 3-115, 4-166, 5-171, 6-173, 7-180, 8-186, 9-193, 10-197.
BOWLING: Ambrose 10-1-24-2, Benjamin 9.4-0-35-0 (w 4), Cummins 10-0-33-4, Simmons 9-0-48-1 (w 1, nb 1) Hooper 10-0-46-1, Arthurton 1-0-5-0.

FALL OF WICKETS: 1-57, 2-81, 3-88, 4-98, 5-112.
BOWLING: Kapil Dev 8-0-45-1, Prabhakar 9-0-55-1 (w 1, nb 1), Raju 10-2-32-1 (w 1), Srinath 9-2-23-2 (nb 3), Tendulkar 3-0-20-0, Srikkanth 1-0-7-0, Jadeja 0.3-0-5-0.

Umpires: SG Randall (Australia) and SJ Woodward (New Zealand).
Man of the Match: AC Cummins
WEST INDIES WON BY FIVE WICKETS

PAKISTAN V AUSTRALIA
World-Class Duffers
Perth, March 11

Pakistan batted first, Sohail and Raja soon showing they wanted to get a move on, and Australia's first embarrassment was the number of wides and no-balls delivered in the opening overs. McDermott, Reid and Waugh between them contributed 15 extras.

Sohail was the star of the side for Pakistan, hitting up 76 off 106 balls, and Javed Miandad scored 46, with Raja scoring 34. Pakistan totalled 220, which seemed at first well within Australia's reach on the fast and true WACA pitch. Yet things started badly for Australia, and grew steadily worse. Moody was out for four and Boon for five, only Marsh, 39, Dean Jones, 47, and Mark Waugh, 30, putting up any resistance.

The last man in, Whitney, reflected the general Australian frustration by exchanging angry words with the wicketkeeper, Moin Khan, and then hitting out at him. Both players were reported for bad behaviour, it being claimed by the Australians that Moin Khan had provoked Whitney verbally. Khan protested that he knew little English. Whitney protested that Khan knew enough to swear at him expertly in English...

In fact it had been an ill-tempered match throughout, both teams no doubt conscious that the loser here was probably out of the tournament running, and at various times there were angry remarks from Boon, Raja, Border and Steve Waugh. It prompted some fans to worry that cricket was getting more like baseball, and that if this kept up we would end up with cricket players actually disagreeing with umpires verbally.

So Australia lost to Pakistan by 48 runs, continuing the run of failures by the defending World Cup champions, who had by this stage lost to New Zealand, South Africa, England and Pakistan. Former Australian captain Ian Chappell chose this stage to criticise coach Bobby Simpson for Australia's plight, saying Allan Border should assert himself as captain and keep Simpson in the background. Calling the Australian team "world class duffers", Chappell said key members of the team had been out of form and shouldn't have been selected. What many felt, however, was that Simon O'Donnell's exclusion from the Australian team was as inexplicable as David Gower's exclusion from the England team.

PAKISTAN		
Aamir Sohail c Healy b Moody		76
Ramiz Raja c Border b Whitney		34
Salim Malik b Moody		0
Javed Miandad c Healy b S R Waugh		46
*Imran Khan c Moody b S R Waugh		13
Inzamam-ul-Haq run out		16
Ijaz Ahmed run out		0
Wasim Akram c M E Waugh b S R Waugh		0
+Moin Khan c Healy b McDermott		5
Mushtaq Ahmed not out		3
Extras (lb 9, w 16, nb 2)		27
TOTAL (9 wkts, 50 overs)		220

Aqib Javed did not bat.
FALL OF WICKETS: 1-78, 2-80, 3-157, 4-193, 5-194, 6-205, 7-205, 8-214, 9-220.
BOWLING: McDermott 10-0-33-1 (w 3), Reid 9-0-37-0 (w 4, nb 2), S R Waugh 10-0-36-3 (w 6), Whitney 10-1-50-1 (w 2), Moody 10-0-42-2 (w 1), M E Waugh 1-0-13-0.

AUSTRALIA		
T M Moody c Malik b Aqib		4
G R Marsh c Khan b Imran		39
D C Boon c Mushtaq b Aqib		5
D M Jones c Aqib b Mushtaq		47
M E Waugh c Ijaz b Mushtaq		30
*A R Border c Ijaz b Mushtaq		1
S R Waugh c Moin b Imran		5
+I A Healy c Ijaz b Aqib		8
C J McDermott lbw b Wasim		0
M R Whitney b Wasim		5
B A Reid not out		0
Extras (lb 7, w 14, nb 7)		28
TOTAL (45.2 overs)		172

FALL OF WICKETS: 1-13, 2-31, 3-116, 4-122, 5-123, 6-130, 7-156, 8-162, 9-167, 10-172.
BOWLING: Wasim 7.2-0-28-2(w 4, nb 3), Aqib 8-1-21-3 (w 6, nb 1), Imran 10-1-32-2, Ijaz 10-0-43-0 (w 4, nb 3), Mushtaq 10-0-41-3.

Umpires: KE Liebenberg (South Africa) and PD Reporter (India).
Man of the Match: Aamir Sohail.
PAKISTAN WON BY 48 RUNS

SOUTH AFRICA v ENGLAND
Light-Years Behind
Melbourne, March 12

The most remarkable cricket stadium in the world, with its capacity for seating 112,000, was a constant fascination, its sheer size awe-inspiring. During this match I wandered to various vantage points including high up in the towering stands where the steep incline of seats almost induced vertigo. It was, at times, like being in a giant open-air opera house.

In this first cricket clash between England and South Africa in more than two decades, Kepler Wessels and Andrew Hudson opened the batting for South Africa and got off to a confident start. Graham Gooch was absent from the England side with a leg injury, but the depth of talent in the England team meant he was hardly missed.

Hudson started positively, stroking the ball to all quarters, and he and Wessels put on 151 runs before Hudson was caught lofting the ball. Wessels was in good form, but the scoring was not as fast as required and Kirsten decided to remedy this by jumping out and lofting a straight six. But in forcing the pace he, too, was soon gone, caught off De Freitas for 11.

Jonty Rhodes was full of purpose as usual, and scored a fast 18 before being run out attempting an impossibly short run. Adrian Kuiper and Hansie Cronje saw out the innings with 15 not out and 13 not out respectively, but in retrospect the South African total of 236 for four should have been at least 260 – the early batsmen not always taking crisp singles that were there for the asking, and the team still tending to over-consolidate in the opening overs.

Ian Botham and Alec Stewart also began confidently, and were in no trouble when rain intervened for 43 minutes, England's innings being reduced to 41 overs and the target to 226. On the resumption, with 62 runs on the board, England lost three quick wickets for only two runs. First McMillan bowled Botham neck, crop and stump-camera, all three stumps being a shambles, with the middle stump (containing the camera) smashed to pieces. In the same over McMillan had Robin Smith caught behind and, a few balls later, Snell had Hick also caught behind.

Hereabouts, however, Wessels made the mistake of resting McMillan and Snell, whose accuracy had been proving a trial and a pressure to Fairbrother and Stewart, and the English pair were able to relax somewhat over the gentler offerings of Kuiper, Cronje and Kirsten. Stewart's innings was perfect for England in the circumstances, and when he was run out for 77, he and Fairbrother, with 75 not out, and Lewis, with 33, had secured the victory for England with one ball to spare.

As with the match against Sri Lanka, it seemed that this was a match South Africa should have won, and could have won if McMillan and Snell had been kept on in both instances. Yet, on the credit side, one sensed a growing toughness and maturity about the South African team. Light-years behind England in one-day experience, they had nevertheless come within one ball of beating the most powerful team in the contest, and could conceivably have won with a measure of ease if they had seized all their opportunities.

Clearly a great deal would now depend on South Africa's match against India in Adelaide in determining whether South Africa would reach the semi-finals.

SOUTH AFRICA	
*K C Wessels c Smith b Hick	85
A C Hudson c and b Hick	79
P N Kirsten c Smith b DeFreitas	11
J N Rhodes run out	18
A P Kuiper not out	15
W J Cronje not out	13
Extras (b 4, lb 4, w 4, nb 3)	15
TOTAL (4 wkts, 50 overs)	236

B M McMillan, +D J Richardson, R P Snell, M W Pringle and A A Donald did not bat.
FALL OF WICKETS: 1-151, 2-170, 3-201, 4-205.
BOWLING: Pringle 9-2-34-0 (w 2, nb 3), DeFreitas 10-1-41-1 (w 1), Botham 8-0-37-0, Small 2-0-14-0 (w 1), Illingworth 10-0-43-0, Reeve 2.4-0-15-0, Hick 8.2-0-44-2.

ENGLAND	
*+A J Stewart run out	77
I T Botham b McMillan	22
R A Smith c Richardson b McMillan	0
G A Hick c Richardson b Snell	1
N H Fairbrother not out	75
D A Reeve c McMillan b Snell	10
C C Lewis run out	33
D R Pringle c Kuiper b Snell	1
P A J DeFreitas not out	1
Extras (lb 3, w 1, nb 2)	6
TOTAL (7 wkts, 40.5 overs)	226

R K Illingworth and G C Small did not bat.
FALL OF WICKETS: 1-63, 2-63, 3-64, 4-132, 5-166, 6-216, 7-225.
BOWLING: Donald 9-1-43-0 (nb 1), Pringle 8-0-44-0 (nb 2, w 1), Snell 7.5-0-42-3, McMillan 8-1-39-2, Kuiper 4-0-32-0, Cronje 3-0-14-0, Kirsten 1-0-9-0.

Umpires: BL Aldridge (New Zealand) and JD Buultjens (Sri Lanka).
Man of the Match: AJ Stewart.
ENGLAND WON BY 3 WICKETS
(England's target reduced to 226 in 41 overs.)

NEW ZEALAND V INDIA
Greatbatch Assaults
Dunedin, March 12

On a bitterly cold day India set about challenging New Zealand's ploy of opening the bowling with slow off-spinner Patel, and sent in Krish Srikkanth to break the spell Patel had been casting over other opening batsmen. The plan was for Srikkanth to annihilate Patel with brilliant aggressive strokeplay, but instead he hit Patel's third ball to Latham at long-on and India were immediately in trouble.

Sachin Tendulkar, the boy genius, teamed with Azharuddin to add 127 runs in 20 overs, Tendulkar ending with 84 and Azharuddin with 55. Kapil Dev, with 33, was the only other Indian batsman to get runs, and the total for six wickets was 230.

There followed another extraordinary Greatbatch assault, featuring four sixes in a whirlwind 73 in 76 balls, three of the sixes off the pace bowling of Kapil Dev. Greatbatch, having reached two 50-ball half-centuries against South Africa and West Indies, reached 50 here off 47 balls and kept New Zealand more than 40 runs ahead of India after 20 overs, maintaining that margin to the finish. Andrew Jones, 67 not out, and Crowe, 26, ensured New Zealand's victory with 17 balls to spare.

INDIA		NEW ZEALAND	
A Jadeja retired hurt	13	MJ Greatbatch c Banerjee b Raju	73
K Srikkanth c Latham b Patel	0	RT Latham b Prabhakar	8
*M Azharuddin c Greatbatch b Patel	55	AH Jones not out	67
S R Tendulkar c Smith b Harris	84	*MD Crowe run out	26
S V Manjrekar c and b Harris	18	+IDS Smith c sub b Prabhakar	9
Kapil Dev c Larsen b Harris	33	KR Rutherford lbw b Raju	21
S Banerjee c Greatbatch b Watson	11	CZ Harris b Prabhakar	4
+K S More not out	2	CL Cairns not out	4
J Srinath not out	4		
Extras (b 1, lb 4, w 4, nb 1)	10	Extras (b 4, lb 3, w 4, nb 8)	19
TOTAL (6 wkts, 50 overs)	230	TOTAL (6 wkts 47.1 overs)	231

M Prabhakar and S L V Raju did not bat.
FALL OF WICKETS: 1-4, 2-149, 3-166, 4-201, 5-222, 6-223.
BOWLING: Cairns 8-1-40-0 (nb 1), Patel 10-0-29-2, Watson 10-1-34-1, Larsen 9-0-43-0, Harris 9-0-55-3 (w 2), Latham 4-0-24-0 (w 2)

DN Patel, GR Larsen and W Watson did not bat.
FALL OF WICKETS: 1-36, 2-118, 3-162, 4-172, 5-206, 6-225
BOWLING: Kapil Dev 10-0-55-0 (w 1, nb 1), Prabhakar 10-0-46-3 (nb 2), Banerjee 6-1-40-0 (nb 1) Srinath 9-0-35-0 (w 2, nb 3), Raju 10-0-38-2 (w 1), Tendulkar 1-0-2-0, Srikkanth 1.1-0-8-0 (nb 1)

Umpires: PJ McConnell (Australia) and ID Robinson (Zimbabwe)
Man of the Match: MJ Greatbatch
NEW ZEALAND WON BY 4 WICKETS

WEST INDIES V SRI LANKA
The Biggest Six
Berri, March 13

In heat and great humidity, West Indies piled up a giant total of 268 in quick time, Phil Simmons smashing up 108 runs with some support from Keith Arthurton, 40, Haynes, 38, and a final partnership between Benjamin and Curtly Ambrose (24 not out and 15 not out respectively) in which Ambrose hit the biggest six ever seen on the ground, straight over the sight-screen.

Sri Lanka, batting, were overwhelmed, being put out for only 177, West Indies winning by 91 runs. Only Samarasekera, 40, and Ranatunga, 24, offered much resistance, Ambrose, Hooper and Arthurton shared the wickets with two each.

WEST INDIES	
DL Haynes c Tillekeratne b Ranatunga	38
BC Lara c and b Ramanayake	1
PV Simmons c Wickremasinghe b Hathurusinghe	110
*RB Richardson run out	8
KLT Arthurton c Tillekeratne b Hathurusinghe	40
AL Logie b Anurasiri	0
CL Hooper c Gurusinha b Hathurusinghe	12
+D Williams c Tillekeratne b Hathurusinghe	2
CEL Ambrose not out	15
WKM Benjamin not out	24
Extras (lb 9, w3, nb 6)	18
TOTAL (8 wkts 50 overs)	268

AC Cummins did not bat.
FALL OF WICKETS: 1-6, 2-72, 3-103, 4-197, 5-199, 6-219, 7-223, 8-228
BOWLING: Wickremasinghe 7-0-30-0 (w 2, nb 1), Ramanayake 7-1-17-1 (w 1, nb 1), Anurasiri 10-0-46-1, Gurusinha 1-0-10-0, Ranatunga 7-0-35-1, Kalpage 10-0-64-0, Hathurusinghe 8-0-57-4 (nb 4).

SRI LANKA	
RS Mahanama c Arthurton b Cummins	11
AR Samarasekera lbw b Hooper	40
UC Hathurusinghe run out	16
*PA de Silva c and b Hooper	11
A Ranatunga c Benjamin b Arthurton	24
AP Gurusinha c Richardson b Ambrose	10
+HP Tillekeratne b Ambrose	3
RS Kalpage not out	13
CP Ramanayake b Arthurton	1
SD Anurasiri b Benjamin	3
GP Wickremasinghe not out	21
Extras (lb 8, w 14, nb2)	24
TOTAL (9 wkts 50 overs)	177

FALL OF WICKETS: 1-56, 2-80, 3-86, 4-99, 5-130, 6-135, 7-137, 8-139, 9-149.
BOWLING: Ambrose 10-2-24-2 (w 6), Benjamin 10-0-34-1 (w 5), Cummins 9-0-49-1 (w 3), Hooper 10-1-19-2, Arthurton 10-0-40-2 (nb 1), Simmons 1-0-3-0, Jadeja 0.3-0-5-0.

Umpires: DR Shepherd (England) and SJ Woodward (New Zealand)
Man of the Match: PV Simmons
WEST INDIES WON BY 91 RUNS

AUSTRALIA v ZIMBABWE
The Brothers Waugh
Hobart, March 14.

After losing Tom Moody to an early run-out, Australia piled up 265 runs with major contributions from Dean Jones, 54, David Boon, 48, and Mark and Steve Waugh, with 66 not out and 55 respectively. Boon, a Tasmanian, received an extra-warm greeting from the home crowd, and the Waugh brothers delighted spectators with their quick-fire century partnership.

Zimbabwe, set more than five runs an hour, lost Shah to a run out for 24, then collapsed, losing five wickets for 41 runs. The best performance for Zimbabwe was a remarkable bowling analysis by veteran John Traicos, the former South African Test off-spinner, who in spite of the Australian onslaught, bowled ten overs for one wicket and only 30 runs.

Australia's easy win, by 128 runs, lifted local spirits and again set commentators speculating on whether Australia might yet steal into the semi-finals by default of some other team.

AUSTRALIA	
TM Moody run out	6
DC Boon b Shah	48
DM Jones b Burmester	54
*AR Border st Flower b Traicos	22
ME Waugh not out	66
SR Waugh b Brandes	55
+IA Healy lbw b Duers	0
PL Taylor not out	1
Extras (b 2, lb 8, n 1, w 2)	13
TOTAL (6 wkts, 46 overs)	265

CJ McDermott, MR Whitney and BA Reid did not bat.

FALL OF WICKETS: 1-8, 2-102, 3-134, 4-144, 5-257, 6-258
BOWLING: Brandes 9-0-59-1 (nb 1), Duers 9-1-48-1 (w 1), Burmester 9-0-65-1 (w 1), Shah 9-0-53-1, Traicos 10-0-30-1

ZIMBABWE	
AH Shah run out	24
+A Flower c Border b SR Waugh	20
AD Campbell c ME Waugh b Whitney	4
AJ Pycroft c ME Waugh b SR Waugh	0
*DL Houghton b McDermott	2
AC Waller c Taylor b Moody	18
KJ Arnott b Whitney	8
EA Brandes c McDermott b Taylor	23
M Burmester c Border b Reid	12
AJ Traicos c Border b Taylor	3
K Duers not out	2
Extras (lb 11, nb 2, w 8)	21
TOTAL (41.4 overs)	137

FALL OF WICKETS: 1-47, 2-51, 3-51, 4-57, 5-69, 6-88, 7-97, 8-117, 9-132, 10-137
BOWLING: McDermott 8-0-26-1 (w 3, nb1), Reid 9-2-17-1 (nb 1), SR Waugh 7-0-28-2 (w 4), Whitney 10-3-15-2, Moody 4-0-25-1 (w 1), Taylor 3.4-0-14-2

Umpires: BR Aldridge (New Zealand) SN Bucknor (West Indies)
Man of the Match: SR Waugh
AUSTRALIA WON BY 128 RUNS

ENGLAND v NEW ZEALAND
Beyond a Fluke
Wellington, March 15.

The long-awaited clash between the two top teams on the points table, played at Basin Reserve in Wellington, got off to a good start for England when Stewart, 41, Smith, 36, and Hick, 56, had England going well ahead of run-rate requirements and poised to plunder off the last 15 overs. But in those last 15 overs England managed only one boundary, having lost seven wickets for 76 runs. Larsen's innocuous-looking medium seamers and Patel's accurate off-cutters had kept the brakes on the Englishmen, and they could manage only 200 runs.

Greatbatch, 35, Andrew Jones, 78, Crowe, 73 not out, took New Zealand to another remarkable victory, this time by seven wickets, and over the very team that had so heavily defeated them only a month before.

Suddenly people were wondering if New Zealand could, after all, be caught out even when playing beyond their shores and away from their slow pitches. Seven wins in seven matches looked beyond a fluke, as sheer luck alone couldn't account for all that success. However, it was still hard to see New Zealand, with a strategy based on only three outstanding players, going right through the tournament unscathed.

ENGLAND	
*+AJ Stewart c Harris b Patel	41
IT Botham b Patel	8
GA Hick c Greatbatch b Harris	56
RA Smith c Patel b Jones	38
AJ Lamb c Cairns b Watson	12
CC Lewis c and b Watson	0
DA Reeve not out	21
DR Pringle c sub (Latham) b Jones	10
PAJ deFreitas c Cairns b Harris	0
RK Illingworth not out	2
Extras (b 1, lb 7, w 4)	12
TOTAL (8 wkts, 50 overs, 186 min)	200

GC Small did not bat.

FALL OF WICKETS: 1-25, 2-95, 3-135, 4-162, 5-162, 6-169, 7-185, 8-195
BOWLING: Patel 10-1-26-2, Harris 8-0-39-2 (w 1), Watson 10-0-40-2 (w 1), Cairns 3-0-21-0 (w 1), Larsen 10-3-24-0 (w 1), Jones 9-0-42-2

NEW ZEALAND	
MJ Greatbatch c DeFreitas b Botham	35
JG Wright b DeFreitas	1
AH Jones run out (Hick)	78
*MD Crowe not out	73
KR Rutherford not out	3
Extras (b 1, lb 8, w 1, nb 1)	11
TOTAL(3 wkts, 40.5 overs, 157 mins)	201

CZ Harris, +IDS Smith, CL Cairns, DN Patel, GR Larsen and W Watson did not bat.
BOWLING: Pringle 6.2-1-34-0 (nb 1, w 1) DeFreitas 8.3-1-45-1, Botham 4-0-19-1, Illingworth 9-1-46-0, Hick 6-0-26-0, Reeve 3-0-9-0, Small 4-0-13-0

Umpires: SG Randall (Australia) and ID Robinson (Zimbabwe)
Man of the Match: AH Jones
NEW ZEALAND WON BY SEVEN WICKETS

INDIA v SOUTH AFRICA
Lofted Unorthodoxies
Adelaide, March 15.

The South African team had enjoyed several days of rest in Adelaide – rest from competitive cricket at any rate – as they prepared to take on India, but the question of the referendum kept obtruding.

Reports in the Australian press and on television seemed to be reflecting a strong right-wing surge in the last few days of the referendum campaign, and it was even being suggested quite openly that the "no" voters would win. Adrian Kuiper, with two small children and a third due soon, was distinctly depressed as he spoke about the possible prospects for his young family. As an apple farmer, he considered the possible re-imposition of sanctions against South African fruit: "My life is international sport and fruit export. If we lose both again, that's it – what could I do?"

Alan Jordaan, the team manager, and Dr. Ali Bacher had talked the whole thing over with the team, and all were agreed they should be publicly identified with the campaign for the "yes" vote.

Geoff Dakin, president of the United Cricket Board of South Africa, went further, and bluntly told South African cricket fans over the transmission from Australia that they could say goodbye to international cricket if the referendum were lost. He also implied the South African team would be withdrawn from the World Cup if the "no" vote won. Certainly the South African players were sufficiently motivated anyway to win against India on purely cricketing grounds, much as they were aware of the political importance of gaining that semi-final place.

Reports of the extent to which their progress was being followed and supported all over South Africa were overwhelming, and as they set out repeatedly for the nets they knew of the high hopes which were riding on their performance.

I felt sorry for Tertius Bosch, the reserve fast bowler who had played only once, on the awful Eden Park wicket, but he was philosophical about being left out and could see the balance of the team required it. A pleasant young man with a ready smile and sunny disposition whose good humour belied his ferocious bowling action, he was at least fortunate at the gaming tables of the casino adjoining our Adelaide hotel, and I was glad the fates had given him some compensation as the day of the vital clash with India dawned.

Persistent drizzle delayed the start for four hours, and the match was reduced to 30 overs a side, India batting first and being the fancied side with their five brilliant attacking batsmen. However, one of these, Srikkanth, went in the first over in a most extraordinary catch. He had slashed a fast ball from Allan Donald over the head of short cover, Peter Kirsten, who jumped high in a leap timed to the split second to clutch the ball one-handed.

Manjrekar and Azharuddin then added 78 runs, taking heavy toll of the normally economical Richard Snell, who conceded 46 runs in only six overs to the rampant Indians. Equally unusually, Adrian Kuiper, who had spent extra grinding hours in the nets, bowled more tightly than every other South African bowler, conceding only 28 runs off his six overs and taking the wickets of Manjrekar, 28, and the brilliant Tendulkar, 14. Kuiper also had a hand in the dismissal of Azharuddin, catching him off Pringle for 79. McMillan also bowled his six overs for 28 – a remarkable achievement against such a talented team of attacking batsmen.

South Africa, set to score 181 runs for victory and a certain place in the semi-final, started with Andrew Hudson and Peter Kirsten, facing a required run-rate of more than six runs per over. Their batting, in the circumstances, was of the highest class as, judiciously mixing aggression with care, they reeled off hooks, pulls, drives glances, cuts and occasional lofted unorthodoxies to beat the field.

The bowling by Kapil Dev, Prabhakar and Tendulkar was accurate and tight, but, when Srinath and Raju bowled, the South Africans accelerated the run rate. Kirsten reached his half-century first, Hudson following soon after, and they posted 128 before Hudson was bowled trying to force the pace.

Adrian Kuiper rapidly added 21 runs with Kirsten before being run out, Jonty Rhodes hitting a big six before being caught square-cutting, and then Kirsten was bowled by Kapil Dev for 84. With two overs to go South Africa needed 14 to win, but Kepler Wessels and Hansie Cronje hit the necessary runs off only seven balls, each smashing a four to the fence, and South Africa had the victory by six wickets – and the hoped-for semi-final place.

INDIA		SOUTH AFRICA	
K Srikkanth c Kirsten b Donald	0	AC Hudson b Srinath	53
SV Manjrekar b Kuiper	28	PN Kirsten b Kapil Dev	84
*M Azharuddin c Kuiper b Pringle	79	AP Kuiper run out	7
SR Tendulkar c Wessels b Kuiper	14	JN Rhodes c Raju b Prabhakar	7
Kapil Dev b Donald	42	*KC Wessels not out	9
VG Kambli run out	1	WJ Cronje not out	8
PK Amre not out	1		
J Srinath not out	0		
Extras (lb 7, w6, nb 2)	15	Extras (lb 10, nb 3)	13
TOTAL: (6 wkts 30 overs)	180	TOTAL (4 wkts, 29.1 overs)	181

M Prabhakar, +KS More and SLV Raju did not bat.

BM McMillan +DJ Richardson, RP Snell, AA Donald and MW Pringle did not bat.

FALL OF WICKETS: 1-1, 2-79, 3-103, 4-174, 5-177, 6-179
BOWLING: Donald 6-0-34-2 (w 3), Pringle 6-0-37-1 (w 2, nb 2), Snell 6-1-46-0, McMillan 6-0-28-0, Kuiper 6-0-28-2 (w 1).

FALL OF WICKETS: 1-128, 2-149, 3-157, 4-163
BOWLING: Kapil Dev 6-0-36-1, Prabhakar 5.1-1-33-1, Tendulkar 6-0-20-0, Srinath 6-0-39-1 (nb 3), Raju 6-0-43-0.

Umpires: JD Buultjens (Sri Lanka) and Khizar Hayat (Pakistan)
Man of the Match: PN Kirsten
SOUTH AFRICA WON BY 6 WICKETS

Overleaf: Pakistan's Kapil Dev and South Africa's Peter Kirsten showed their hitting powers.

SRI LANKA v PAKISTAN
An Expensive Drop
Perth, March 15.

Sri Lanka batted first, reaching 212 runs for six wickets with Aravinda da Silva, 43, top-scoring, supported by Samarasekera, 38, Gurusinha, 37, and Tillekeratne, 25 not out. Not normally a bad total, this now seemed inadequate in the face of the strong Pakistani batting and the relatively weak Sri Lankan bowling. For Pakistan, the bowling honours went to Wasim Akram, 10 overs for 37, to Aqib Javed, 10 overs for 39, and to Imran Khan, whose eight overs cost 36. The 21-year-old Mushtaq Ahmed showed for the second time in five days that good legspin could be a positive factor in one-day cricket, finishing with two wickets for 43 in ten overs.

Replying, Pakistan at first slumped to 84 for three, but Javed Miandad, 57, and Salim Malik, 51, added 101 runs in the next 21 overs, and Wasim Akram and Ijaz Ahmed saw Pakistan home by four wickets. Sri Lanka's chance to record their third win of the tournament was probably lost when Javed Miandad was dropped earlier at mid-wicket.

Australians tended to see Pakistan's win as a further set-back to their own hopes of reaching the semi-final, though it still remained possible for any one of three teams – Australia, West Indies or Pakistan – to join England, New Zealand and South Africa in the final four.

SRI LANKA	
RS Mahanama b Wasim Akram	12
MAR Samarasekera st Moin b Mushtaq	38
UC Hathurusinghe b Mushtaq	5
*PA de Silva c Sohail b Ijaz	43
AP Gurusinha c Malik b Imran	37
A Ranatunga c sub (Zahid) b Sohail	7
+HP Tillekeratne not out	25
RS Kalpage not out	13
Extras (lb 15, nb 6, w 1)	32
TOTAL (6 wkts 50 overs)	212

HCP Ramanayake, GP Wickremasinghe and KIJ Wijegunawardene did not bat.
FALL OF WICKETS: 1-29, 2-48, 3-99, 4-132, 5-158, 6-187
BOWLING: Wasim 10-0-37-1 (w 2, nb 4), Aqib 10-0-39-0 (w 3, nb 2) Imran 8-1-36-1, Mushtaq 10-0-43-2 (w 2), Ijaz 8-0-28-1 (w 3), Aamir 4-0-14-1 (w 1).

PAKISTAN	
Aamir Sohail c Mahanama b Ramanayake	1
Rameez Raja c Gurusinha b Wickremasinghe	32
Javed Miandad c Wickremasinghe b Gurusinha	57
*Imran Khan c De Silva b Hathurusinghe	22
Salim Malik c Kalpage b Ramanayake	51
Inzamam-ul-Haq run out	11
Ijaz Ahmed not out	8
Wasim Akram not out	5
Extras (lb 12, w 9, nb 8)	29
TOTAL (wkt 6, 49.1 overs)	216

+Moin Khan, Mushtaq Ahmed and Aqib Javed did not bat
FALL OF WICKETS: 1-7, 2-68, 3-84, 4-185, 5-201, 6-205
BOWLING: Wijegunawardene 10-1-34-0 (nb 7), Ramanayake 10-1-37-2 (w 4), Wickremasinghe 9.1-0-41-1 (w 1), Gurusinha 9-0-38-1 (w 1), Hathurusinghe 9-0-40-1 (w 2), Kalpage 2-0-14-0 (w 1).

Umpires: KE Liebenberg (South Africa) and PJ McConnell (Australia)
Man of the Match: Javed Miandad
PAKISTAN WON BY 4 WICKETS

NEW ZEALAND V PAKISTAN
Ramiz takes Root
Christchurch, March 18.

The remaining three matches, Australia v. West Indies, England v. Zimbabwe, and Pakistan v. New Zealand, would decide not only which of West Indies, Pakistan or Australia would join the top three in the semi-finals, but which of the semi-finalists would play each other, since the rules called for the top team to play the fourth and the second to play the third; the two winners of these matches would contest the final.

The overall position, then, by the middle of March, was as follows:

	Played	Won	Lost	Drew	Points
New Zealand	7	7	—	—	14
England	7	5	1	1	11
South Africa	8	5	3	—	10
West Indies	7	4	3	—	8
Pakistan	7	3	3	1	7
Australia	7	3	4	—	6
India	8	2	5	1	5
Sri Lanka	8	2	5	—	5
Zimbabwe	7	—	7	—	0

At this stage Peter Kirsten had maintained his position as top-scoring batsman of the 1992 World Cup. Despite having missed one match through injury, he had the top aggregate of 399 runs and an average of 79.80 with four half centuries. His scores to date were:

Against Australia	49 not out
Against New Zealand	90
Against Sri Lanka	47
Against West Indies	56
Against Zimbabwe	62 not out
Against England	11
Against India	84

Considering that he was not initially chosen for the team, many wondered how the other two stars not chosen, Cook and Rice, would have fared in this World Cup.

Pakistan won the toss and put New Zealand in to bat in this key match – "key" in that victory could put Pakistan into the semi-finals, whereas defeat could mean that Australia might still sneak in by beating West Indies.

Wasim Akram soon removed Jones and Crowe, and Aqib got rid of Latham, but when Greatbatch hit Aqib for four, six and four from successive deliveries, Imran replaced him with the young legspinner, Mushtaq Ahmed. The new arrival first constricted Greatbatch, then had him caught, finishing with two wickets for 18 runs in ten overs.

Wasim, for his part, ended with four wickets for 32 off nine overs, New Zealand being dismissed for 166 – their first poor total of the tournament. Pakistan then suffered their own shocks, losing two quick wickets to Danny Morrison – Sohail and Ul-Haq – before Ramiz Raja took root and, with help from Javed Miandad, carried Pakistan to victory.

Ramiz scored 119 not out, Pakistan winning by seven wickets to inflict New Zealand's first defeat of the tournament.

The news was glumly received in Melbourne, where Australia were playing West Indies; they now realised their last hope of making the semi-final was gone, regardless of their own result.

NEW ZEALAND

MJ Greatbatch c Salim b Mushtaq	42
RT Latham c Inzamam b Aqib	6
AH Jones b Akram	2
*MD Crowe c Aamir b Akram	3
KR Rutherford run out	8
CZ Harris st Moin b Mushtaq	1
DN Patel c Mushtaq c Sohail	7
+IIDS Smith b Imran	1
GR Larsen b Akram	37
DK Morrison c Malik b Akram	12
W Watson not out	5
Extras (b 3, lb 23, nb 4, w 12)	42
TOTAL (48.2 overs)	166

PAKISTAN

Aamir Sohail c Patel b Morrison	0
Ramiz Raja not out	119
Inzamam-ul-Haq b Morrison	5
Javed Miandad lbw b Morrison	30
Salim Malik not out	9
Extras (1 lb, 2 nb, w 1)	4
TOTAL: (3wkts 44.4 overs)	167

FALL OF WICKETS: 1-23, 2-26, 3-39, 4-85, 5-88, 6-93, 7-96, 8-106, 9-150, 10-166
BOWLING: Wasim 9.2-0-32-4,(w9,nb2) Aqib 10-1-34-1(w2,nb1) Mushtaq 10-2-18-2(w1) Imran 8-0-22-1(nb1) Aamir 10-1-29-1 Ijaz 1-0-5-0.

Ijaz Ahmed, *Imran Khan, Wasim Akram, +Moin Khan, Mushtaq Ahmed and Aqib Javed did not bat.
FALL OF WICKETS: 1-0, 2 -9, 3-124
BOWLING: Morrison 10-0-42-3 (nb 2), Patel 10-2-25-0, Watson 10-3-26-0, Harris 4-0-18-0, Larsen 3-0-16-0, Jones 3-0-10-0, Latham 2-0-13-0, Rutherford 1.4-0-11-0 (w 1), Greatbatch 1-0-5-0.

Umpires: SN Bucknor (West Indies) and SG Randall (Australia)
Man of the Match: Mushtaq Ahmed
PAKISTAN WON BY 7 WICKETS

AUSTRALIA v WEST INDIES
Out of the Running
Melbourne, March 18.

Realising they were playing for pride and no longer for position, the Australians put up their best start in many matches, David Boon and Tom Moody compiling 107 for the first wicket. But then Australia lost Moody, Jones, Border and Steve Waugh in quick succession, and although a total of 216 was reached – largely through Boon's century – one felt that capital had not been made of the good start.

When West Indies batted it was soon obvious that Brian Lara was in superb form, playing elegant strokes all round the wicket. But here, finally, the Australian bowlers got their act together and applied real pressure through consistent accuracy.

It was bitter for West Indies, as they had to win to reach the semi-final, but Reid, with 10 overs for 26 runs, McDermott, with two wickets from six overs, and Whitney, with four for 34 off ten overs, made the run rate impossible, and the West Indians contributed to their own defeat with two silly runouts – one of which cost Lara his wicket when he was on 70 and batting brilliantly.

So Australia won by 57 runs, bowing out of the tournament with some pride; and West Indies, with little consolation, were now also out of the running.

AUSTRALIA	
TM Moody c Benjamin b Simmons	42
DC Boon c Williams b Cummins	100
DM Jones c Williams b Cummins	6
*AR Border lbw b Simmons	8
ME Waugh st Williams b Hooper	21
SR Waugh b Cummins	6
+IA Healy not out	11
PL Taylor not out	10
Extras (lb 3, w 3, nb 6)	12
TOTAL (6 wkts, 50 overs)	216

BA Reid, MR Whitney and CR McDermott did not bat
FALL OF WICKETS: 1-107, 2-128, 3-141, 4-185, 5-189, 6-200
BOWLING: Ambrose 10-0-46-0 (w 2, nb 6), Benjamin 10-1-49-0, Cummins 10-1-38-3, Hooper 10-0-40-0 (w 1), Simmons 10-1-40-2

WEST INDIES	
DL Haynes c Jones b McDermott	14
BC Lara run out	70
PV Simmons lbw b McDermott	0
*RB Richardson c Healy b Whitney	10
KLT Arthurton c McDermott b Whitney	15
AL Logie c Healy b Whitney	5
CL Hooper c M Waugh b Whitney	4
+D Williams c Border b Reid	4
WKM Benjamin lbw b S Waugh	15
CEL Ambrose run out	2
A Cummins not out	5
Extras (b 3, lb 5, w 3, nb 4)	15
TOTAL: (42.2 overs)	159

FALL OF WICKETS: 1-27, 2-27, 3-59, 4-83, 5-99, 6-117, 7-128, 8-137, 9-150, 10-159
BOWLING: McDermott 6-1-29-2 (nb 3), Reid 10-1-26-1, Whitney 10-1-34-4, SR Waugh 6.4-0-24-1, Taylor 4-0-24-0, Moody 6-1-14-0 (w 1)

Umpires: PD Reporter (India) and DR Shepherd (England)
Man of the Match: DC Boon
AUSTRALIA WON BY 57 RUNS

ZIMBABWE v ENGLAND
A Memorable Victory
Albury, March 18.

The semi-final teams and venues were now all known. New Zealand would play Pakistan in Auckland, and South Africa would play England in Sydney,. But meanwhile, England were having some unexpected problems against Zimbabwe...

At first, all proceeded according to expectations in this match, the England bowlers dismissing Zimbabwe for a paltry 134 – Ian Botham being the dominant bowler with three for 23 in 10 overs. And when England started batting Botham again dominated, scoring 18 as an opener before a succession of wickets began to tumble. By the time England had lost five wickets for 43 runs, the unthinkable began to seem possible – would Zimbabwe beat England as They had beaten Australia nine years ago?

Eddo Brandes, with four for 21 off 10 overs, Ali Shah, with two for 17 in ten overs, and the amazing John Traicos, bowling with absolute precision for sixteen off ten overs, had support from Jarvis and Butchart, and the Zimbabweans actually did the unthinkable – putting England out for 125 to give Zimbabwe a memorable nine run victory.

England, with two surprise defeats in successive matches, had a slightly tarnished image as the semi-final teams headed for their respective venues. The semi-finals were, in fact, wide open – any of the four teams could go through to take the World Cup.

ZIMBABWE		ENGLAND	
WR James c and b Illingworth	13	*GA Gooch lbw Brandes	0
+A Flower b DeFreitas	7	IT Botham c Flower b Shah	18
AJ Pycroft c Gooch b Botham	3	AJ Lamb c James b Brandes	17
KJ Arnott lbw b Botham	11	RA Smith b Brandes	2
*DL Houghton c Fairbrother b Small	29	GA Hick b Brandes	0
AC Waller b Tufnell	8	NH Fairbrother c Flower b Butchart	20
AH Shah c Lamb b Tufnell	3	+AJ Stewart c Waller b Shah	29
IP Butchart c Fairbrother b Botham	24	PAJ DeFreitas c Flower b Butchart	4
EA Brandes st Stewart b Illingworth	14	RK Illingworth run out (Pycroft)	11
AJ Traicos not out	0	GC Small c Pycroft b Jarvis	5
MP Jarvis lbw b Illingworth	6	PCR Tufnell not out	0
Extras (lb 8, w 8)	16	Extras: (b 4, lb 3, nb 1, w 11)	19
TOTAL: (46.1 overs, 182 min)	134	TOTAL: (49.1 overs, 200 min)	125

FALL OF WICKETS: 1-12, 2-19, 3-30, 4-52, 6-77, 7-96, 8-127, 9-127, 10-134
BOWLING: DeFreitas 8-1-14-1(w 2), Small 9-1-20-1 (w 1), Botham10-2-23-3 (w 4), Illingworth 9.1-0-33-3, Tufnell 10-2-36-2 (w 1).

FALL OF WICKETS: 1-0, 2-32, 3-42, 4-42, 5-43, 6-95, 7-101, 8-108, 9-124, 10-125
BOWLING: Brandes 10-4-21-4, Jarvis 9.1-0-32-1 (w 2), Shah 10-3-17-2 (w 3), Traicos 10-4-16-0, Butchart 10-2-32-2 (w 6, nb 1).

Umpires: BR Aldridge (New Zealand) and Khizar Hayat (Pakistan)

Man of the Match: EA Brandes

ZIMBABWE WON BY 9 RUNS

THE FIRST SEMIFINAL
NEW ZEALAND v PAKISTAN
The Triumph of Inzamam Ul-Haq
Auckland, March 21

Pakistan took a bold approach to this second contest against New Zealand in Auckland, picking two legspinners – Mushtaq Ahmed and Iqbal Sikander. It seemed almost eccentric in a sport in which most teams shudder at the prospect of risking even one legspinner. Batting first, New Zealand started well, Greatbatch and Wright cruising to 35 without undue problems and with Greatbatch, in particular, looking set to explode at any moment into one of his frenzied innings. But Aqib Javed bowled him out with a perfectly slowed delivery and Mushtaq Ahmed came on to bowl.

He immediately pinned the batsmen down while making them look slightly foolish in their inability to pick his googly and topspinner. One leg-break delivered to Jones spun so vastly past his bat that it also beat wicketkeeper Moin and went for byes. With a kind of inevitability Mushtaq eventually frustrated Wright into lofting him straight to Ramiz Raja in the deep. At this stage Martin Crowe came in to bat with such class, such obvious ease of execution and with so much time to play his strokes (while his partner was in such obvious difficulty) that one realised afresh how pre-eminent he and Peter Kirsten had been in this tournament. Wherever the ball pitched, Crowe had the right stroke for it, and he began inexorably to accelerate the run rate. Suddenly with the score on 87, Jones was trapped lbw by Mushtaq after having been tormented and constricted by the young legspinner, and Rutherford came in to join his captain. It was during the consequent partnership of over a hundred between Crowe and Rutherford that one sensed New Zealand were taking a conclusive grip on this game which would see them into the final. Rutherford began cautiously, taking a long look at the pitch and the bounce and pace of the ball, then started lashing out in all directions, and he and Crowe did as they liked for a good half hour. Then Wasim Akram struck suddenly, Rutherford edging the ball to Moin behind the stumps, and Chris Harris came in to join Crowe.

Here, again, one felt while watching Crowe that one was seeing one of the very best batsmen in the world and one of New Zealand's best of all time. But just as the thought was registering, Crowe slumped in agony, having torn a hamstring. It was a major blow for New Zealand – for even if they won their way into the final, they would be without their captain and star player in what they hoped would be the great Melbourne showdown. Greatbatch came out to run for him, but in one of those typical runner's mix-ups was run out, Crowe's innings ending on 91.

However, veteran wicketkeeper and unorthodox slogger Ian Smith came in to rattle up a quickfire 18, making many wonder why he hadn't been sent in earlier in the circumstances. Nevertheless New Zealand had added 143 in their last 16 overs, with 81 coming off the final ten, setting Pakistan the formidable task of reaching 263 to win at a strike rate of more than five runs per over. Martin Crowe, meanwhile, was out of all further participation in the World Cup, having been named Player of the Tournament. It seemed too great a target for Pakistan as Aamir Sohail went for only 14, caught sweeping Patel, and Rameez Raja was caught off Watson for 44, and although Imran Khan and Javed Miandad held the fort for an hour at this point, consolidating the innings, they were falling seriously behind the required run rate, and when both Imran and Salim Malik were caught for 44 and 1 respectively, Pakistan had lost four top-order batsmen for only 140 runs, and were well behind the target and the rate.

Then began one of the most extraordinary innings in the history of the World Cup. The twenty-two year-old Inzamam Ul-Haq turned the entire game around within half an hour of brilliant attack. He drove like lightning along the grass, he lofted with contemptuous disdain. He off-drove one enormous six deep into the crowd on the terraces, then hooked and swept fours off the line of the off-stump. Within two overs the New Zealanders didn't know where to bowl to him – but wherever they pitched he pursued and smashed the ball with uncanny control. Suddenly it was no longer a defensive rearguard action for Pakistan but triumphant dash to victory. When Inzamam was run out for 60 off 37 balls the rest seemed formality.

Javed Miandad, with 57 not out, helped mainly by Moin Khan, with 20 not out, reached their goal with an over and four wickets to spare. Pakistan had snatched victory from what had looked like certain defeat. Now they were heading triumphantly for the final at Melbourne against the winner of the other semi-final at Melbourne South Africa and England.

Critics were taking a second look at the young stars of the Pakistan team – especially the twenty-two year-olds; Ul-Haq, Mushtaq Ahmed and Moin Khan – and reflecting how many World Cups of the future would be adorned by their flowering talent.

NEW ZEALAND		PAKISTAN	
M J Greatbatch b Aqib	17	Aamir Sohail c Jones b Patel	14
J G Wright c Ramiz b Mushtaq	13	Ramiz Raja c Morrison b Watson	44
A H Jones lbw b Mushtaq	21	*Imran Khan c Larsen b Harris	44
*M D Crowe run out	91	Javed Miandad not out	57
K R Rutherford c Moin b Akram	50	Salim Malik c sub (Latham) b Larsen	1
C Z Harris st Moin b Sikander	13	Inzamam ul-Haq run out	60
+I D S Smith not out	18	Wasim Akram b Watson	9
D N Patel lbw Akram	8	+Moin Khan not out	20
G R Larsen not out	8		
Extras (b 4, lb 7, w 8 , nb 4)	23	Extras (b 4, lb 10, w 1)	15
TOTAL (7 wkts, 50 overs, 209 mins)	262	TOTAL (6 wkts 50 overs)	264

D K Morrison, W Watson did not bat.

Aqib Javed, Mushtaq Ahmed and Iqbal Sikander did not bat.

FALL OF WICKETS: 1-35, 2-39, 3-87, 4-194, 5-214, 6-221

FALL OF WICKETS: 1-30, 2-84, 3-134, 4-140, 5-227, 6-238

BOWLING: Wasim Akram 10-0-40-2 (nb 4, w 2), Aqib Javed 10-2-45-1 (w 2), Mushtaq Ahmed 10-0-40-2, Imran Khan 10-0-59 (w 3), Iqbal Sikander 9-0-56-1 (w 1), Iqbal Sikander 9-0-56-1 (w 1).

BOWLING: D Patel 10-1-50-1, D Morrison 9-0-55-0 (w 1), Watson 10-2-39-2, G Larsen 10-1-34-1, C Harris 10-0-72-1

Umpires: SN Bucknor (West Indies), DR Shepherd (England)

Man of the Match: Inzamam Ul-Haq

PAKISTAN WON BY FOUR WICKETS

SECOND SEMI-FINAL

ENGLAND v SOUTH AFRICA
A Mockery of the Game
Sydney, March 22

For the South African team, dreams were coming true all over the place. Following their dramatic win over India in Adelaide, in a run-chase reaching more than six per over, had come the referendum back in South Africa, which, after looming over the heads of the team, had sent them into high delight with its outcome.

It was easy to be cool now, but on the day of the vote there had been tense faces among many in the South African party, whether players, supporters or media representatives, with last-minute panic predictions in the Australian press of a late surge of right-wing support in South Africa.

In several Australian television interviews I had predicted a 55% yes vote, adding that I would settle for a 51% win, so when the outcome proved to be a 68% yes-vote we were all ecstatic You could see the exhilaration on the faces of the cricketers.

Still, nobody underestimated the huge challenge ahead in the semi-final against England. England were still the highest rated team in the tournament, being strongest on paper even without the great left-hander David Gower. England had a potential batting line-up right down to number eleven, depending on what permutation they chose, although the inherent lack of imagination in English selection would incline them to choose the extra bowler.

Personally I would have chosen Gooch, Botham, Stewart, Smith, Hick, Fairbrother, Lamb, Lewis, Reeve, De Freitas and Illingworth, my bowling being handled by Botham, De Freitas, Lewis, Hick, Reeve and Illingworth. In the event the England selectors brought in Gladstone Small in place of Smith, so they now had eight bowlers ...

South Africa won the toss and put England in to bat under a threatening sky with clouds low over a full Sydney Cricket Ground – one of the reasons why I thought they should have batted. Under the bizarre rain rule of this tournament, which decides a target by the highest-scoring overs, the side batting second is always greatly disadvantaged, and this match was already starting ten minutes late because of showers.

However, in spite of the usual spraying of a few wides, the South African fast bowlers struck early again. Gooch was caught behind off Donald, beaten by sheer pace. Donald was whipping his arm over like a blur, and the ball was whistling through to wicketkeeper Richardson. His speed here was additional evidence that he was the fastest bowler in the tournament.

At the other end Meyrick Pringle was also whipping them down at scarcely less speed than Donald, and he caused Botham to chop the ball on his stumps just when the great all-rounder, having played confidently for 21, appeared set for a major innings.

Stewart and Hick dug in after early scares. Pringle twice dismissed Hick only to be no-balled for over-reaching the delivery line. After several overs of South African dominance both Hick and Stewart began to play some attractive attacking strokes. Hick

141

in particular showed the sort of ominous timing he has manifested in his mammoth county innings such as his 405 not out against Somerset.

England seemed to be past the safety point of innings consolidation when the ever-reliable Brian McMillan broke the partnership, his extra bounce and impressive speed getting Stewart caught behind for 33. Snell, also bowling very fast, got one to rise outside the off stump. Hick chopped it like lightning to point, where the adhesive hands of Jonty Rhodes fastened on to it as he jumped skyward in delight, hurling the ball aloft while in the air with heels high like a Cossack dancer.

Meyrick Pringle, returning from the Paddington end, sent a very fast ball right through Fairbrother's 'gate' to demolish his stumps. This ball was one of the best of the tournament, being almost unplayable. It pitched on Fairbrother's off stump, seaming in to take his middle and leg stumps.

At this stage, with five wickets down, by all reasonable cricketing expectations, England should have looked somewhat vulnerable, but so long was this batting line-up that batsmen of the talent of Allan Lamb and Chris Lewis lay in wait at numbers six and seven, with potential century makers down to Illingworth at number ten.

Lamb added a quick 19 before being caught behind off Donald, and Lewis, 18 not out, and Reeve, 25 not out, saw England through to the end of the forty-fifth over, Reeve being a revelation of batting improvisation, scoring his runs off only the few last balls. The innings was truncated by five overs by the umpires because South Africa had fallen short of delivering its fifty overs in the time allocated, so South Africa now had the daunting target of 253 off only 45 overs at a required run rate of around six per over.

Wessels and Hudson began brilliantly. Wessels, not previously seen in such aggressive mood in this tournament, blazed 17 runs off the first few overs before he failed to keep down a square cut off Botham and was caught at point by Lewis. Batsmen are often trapped by apparently innocuous short balls by Botham. What undoes them is the extra bounce he often achieves. Wessels stayed on the field to act as runner for the injured Kirsten, who had strained a muscle in his leg while fielding.

Kirsten and Hudson added 35 runs with some attractive attacking shots, though it was clear that Kirsten was hampered in his movements, and Hudson in particular was again looking a batsman of class with a full range of crisp attacking strokes.

With 61 runs on the board in quick time, Kirsten was beaten and bowled by a beauty of an outswinger from De Freitas, bringing in Kuiper, a batsman of rare attacking gifts who alone would swing this match South Africa's way within thirty to forty minutes.

Kuiper hadn't really fired on all cylinders in any of his innings in this tournament and there was a general feeling that this was the moment for him to 'explode'. Deeply conscious of this, Kuiper had probably been over-anxious to bat well, though he had turned in some of the team's best bowling performances as a medium-fast seamer.

Kuiper took time to look the bowling over, then began to play some shots of impressive authority, especially through the covers and to the on, and watchers began to sense that if he truly opened his shoulders the ball would travel prodigious distances.

In fact, Kuiper decided to take on Illingworth and hoisted him high back over his head, hitting the sight-screen. He repeated the shot several balls later, and appeared to be getting into his stride, though it was off the quicker bowling that he began to lash some lofted fours, including one to the mid-off boundary.

Hudson, who had run to an impressive 46 and looked set for a major innings, was trapped lbw by Illingworth, who then had another notable success when Kuiper jumped out to hoist him over the M. A. Noble Stand, missed, and was bowled.

This brought the two youngsters of the team together, Cronje and Jonty Rhodes, both aged 22. Both played with an astonishing degree of maturity in judgement of runs and strokes, allied to fleetness of foot in taking short singles that appeared to make run-outs impossible of achievement.

These two added 46 before Cronje's lofted legside hit was held in the deep by Graham Hick, whose capacious hands seem as adhesive as Jonty Rhodes's.

Rhodes, joined by McMillan, stepped up the attack and began flogging the ball with exceptional power to all quarters, looking capable of emulating Ul-Haq's feat for the Pakistanis. He and Macmillan had added a very fast 30 runs when Rhodes side-edged an offside slash and found Chris Lewis waiting at deep cover – another of cricket's outstanding fielders and catchers.

David Richardson joined McMillan and the assault on the run-rate continued to a stage where, with two overs and one ball left to get 22 runs for victory with four wickets in hand, play was stopped by the umpires, who felt that a rain shower had become too heavy for play to continue.

This was certainly a tenable ruling in most circumstances, though not, I believe in this one. The teams had stayed on the field through two previous showers when England had batted, and it would have been in the much-vaunted spirit of cricket if Gooch had consented to play through the remaining 13 balls.

But the bizarre rain rules now resulted in the deduction of two overs from the lost twelve minutes of play before the showers stopped and the players returned, with the preposterous consequence that instead of having thirteen balls to score 22 runs, McMillan and Richardson now had one ball in which to score 21!

Again the concept of umpiring had been misunderstood, and literal regulations allowed precedence over natural fairness to make a mockery of a game meant to be the essence of fair play.

Fair play or no, England won by 19 runs to go into the final, and the South Africans, like the New Zealanders the day before in Auckland, sportingly congratulated their victors, then set off on a lap around the Sydney Cricket Ground to thank the capacity crowd for its support. The applause as they jogged around the circuit, waving, was deafening, and was as much a heartfelt welcome back to international cricket as it was an acknowledgement of the quality of their play.

The crowd throughout had been outrightly hostile to England. A century-old rivalry seemed to have coalesced with recent controversies involving the Queen and the Australian premier. The unfortunate England team were booed and jeered throughout this match as a matter of principle. Only one section of the stadium, near the former Hill, was crammed with England supporters who sang and shouted their support throughout the match.

In fact the behaviour of the crowd at the end of the match was somewhat alarming, with debris of all kinds, including bottles, raining down on to the field on quite a wide front, not just from a raucous corner. The action of the South Africans in ostentatiously shaking hands with the English players out on the field did much to defuse the potential nastiness of the moment, as did their spontaneous lap around the field.

The scoreboard reflecting the absurdity of the rain rules.

After all, the rules that had just made a mockery of the game had been drawn up in Australia, and could hardly be blamed on the English team. The South Africans certainly weren't blaming them for the rules, and pointed out that in Melbourne the rain-delay rule had actually favoured South Africa over England, although it hadn't been as grotesquely applied nor as inappropriate to a semi-final match in the World Cup.

Admittedly Gooch could have declined the umpires' offers to go off when the rain came, on the basis that the batsmen were unlikely to reach the target. On the other hand, Richardson and McMillan were looking like the good batsmen they were, and were starting to improvise ...

In fairness, the England team had looked more professional and more powerful from the first over to near the end, and it was only in the final overs that South Africa looked capable of winning, given a stroke or two of luck. England probably deserved to win – but it would have been nice to see the match resolved in the spirit of cricket. Cricket itself would have benefited more from playing out those final thirteen balls.

Geoff Halbish, general manager of the Australian Cricket Board, defended the umpires' handling of the decision and the rules themselves. He said 4.2 minutes were deducted for each over and the match had to finish at 10.10 because the meal break had been reduced after the match started ten minutes late.

He said the playing time couldn't be extended because the team bowling second should not be penalised for bowling their overs quickly, South Africa having bowled their 45 overs in 210 minutes.

True enough, and the rule had earlier benefited South Africa in Brisbane against Pakistan and in Melbourne against England, but Mr Halbish should have given the real reason why play couldn't be extended past 10.10 – because it wouldn't have suited Channel 9 and their programme schedules.

In this case the schedules won, and cricket lost.

ENGLAND		SOUTH AFRICA	
*GA Gooch c Richardson b Donald	2	*KC Wessels c Lewis b Botham	17
IT Botham b Pringle	21	AC Hudson lbw b Illingworth	46
+AJ Stewart c Richardson b McMillan	33	PN Kirsten b DeFreitas	11
GA Hick c Rhodes b Snell	83	WJ Cronje c Hick b Small	24
NH Fairbrother b Pringle	28	AP Kuiper b Illingworth	36
AJ Lamb c Richardson b Donald	19	JN Rhodes c Lewis b Small	43
CC Lewis not out	18	BM McMillan not out	21
DA Reeve not out	25	+DJ Richardson not out	13
Extras (b 1, lb 6, w 13)	13	Extras (lb 17, w4)	21
TOTAL (9 wkts, 214 min, 50 overs)	252	TOTAL (6 wkts 43 overs)	232

PAJ DeFreitas, RK Illingworth and GC Small did not bat
FALL OF WICKETS: 1-20, 2-39, 3-110, 4-183, 5-187, 6-221
BOWLING: Donald 10-0-69-2 (w 5, nb 2), Pringle 9-2-36-2 (w 5 nb 2), Snell 8-0-52-1 (w 2), McMillan 9-0-47-1, Kuiper 5-0-26-0, Cronje 4-0-14-0

RP Snell, MW Pringle and AA Donald did not bat
FALL OF WICKETS: 1-26, 2-61, 3-90, 4-131, 5-176, 6-206
BOWLING: Botham 10-0-52-1, Lewis 5-0-38-0, DeFreitas 8-1-28-1 (w 1), Illingworth 10-1-46-2, Small 10-1-51-2

Umpires: BR Aldridge (New Zealand) and SG Randall (Australia)
Man of the Match: GA Hick
ENGLAND WON BY 19 RUNS

... So the scene was set for the final, in Melbourne – England versus Pakistan – which promised to be a fascinating contest of varying skills and strengths.

THE FINAL
PAKISTAN v ENGLAND
Beware the Wrath of Khan
Melbourne, March 25

It was fitting that the 1992 World Cup should be decided in this vast stadium symbolising the premier venue in the Antipodes – the 115,000-seater Melbourne Cricket Ground where a record attendance for a one-day match was expected of around 90,000 despite the fact that Australia was out of the contest. I looked out of my hotel window across Yarra Park in the early morning, and the stadium looked like a huge circular spacecraft emerging from the misty treetops, with the the four towering floodlight pods resembling the cobra-like firing devices in Wells's War of the Worlds.

Although the match was due to start only at 2.30 crowds started streaming in as early as noon, and by the time I had walked across from the hotel an hour before start of play more than 65,000 were already in their seats. Later a further 20,000 streamed in and the final official attendance figure clocked through the turnstiles was 87,182.

It was already obvious that most of these were keenly supporting Pakistan – anyone but the much-resented Poms. And fuel had been added to the Oz-Pom fire the night before when England captain Graham Gooch and Ian Botham had walked out of an official World Cup banquet in protest because an Australian comedian there had during the staged cabaret entertainment impersonated the Queen in what they regarded as an insulting manner. It was hard to imagine anything more insulting towards the Queen than British television's Spitting Image series, but maybe Botham and Gooch were just bored with the Banquet.

Imran Khan won the toss and chose to bat, as one of the banners in the Pakistani section of the crowd warned: 'Beware the Wrath of Khan!'

Nevertheless, for the next two hours the match appeared to be going one-sidedly England's way as Pakistan lost two quick wickets then appeared mired in a low scoring rate. Aamir Sohail and Ramiz Raja both fell to Derek Pringle, who opened the bowling with Lewis. Sohail was caught behind by Stewart for four and Ramiz went lbw for eight.

And as Ian Botham and De Freitas kept the lid tight on the run-rate on taking over the bowling from Pringle and Lewis, Imran Khan and Javed Miandad became bogged down until close to the 30th over, when in the final hour they began to assert themselves. Imran especially played some fine lofted shots to break England's bowling stranglehold. Hitting out with increasing freedom, the two Pakistani veterans hoisted the total to 163 before being parted, Botham getting Imran for a fine 72, caught calmly in the deep by Illingworth. Botham then returned the compliment to Illingworth, catching Javed Miandad off him, and at 197 for four Pakistan hadn't yet got out of trouble.

But then followed a remarkable onslaught by young Inzamam Ul-Haq and Wasim Akram who sent the score soaring, Wasim actually dominating the latter stages with some vigorous left-handed hitting before being run out for 33. Ul-Haq again impressed hugely from the first ball he received, scoring at will with a wide variety of strokes and reaching the boundary with effortless glances, drives and placements. He cruised with astonishing speed into the forties, then, strangely, became less effective as he switched from strokeplay to crass slogging in the last overs, being out to the crudest of cross-batted slashes, bowled Pringle.

Pringle had finished with the remarkable analysis of 10 overs, 22 runs and three wickets, all the others having been savaged by the latter-stage onslaught of the Pakistanis. Still, while 249 was a handy total it was far from beyond the reach of the powerful England batting line-up. In my opinion the line-up could have been stronger, but Gooch, it seemed, felt insecure without about seven bowlers. I felt that Mark Ramprakash would have been invaluable with the bat and in the field, and I would have wanted to play even a half-fit Smith for his batting.

Imran Khan, captain of Pakistan.

During the Pakistani innings I made an interesting discovery – that the man on my left in the press box, Mr Laurence Costin, was doing all the public announcements for this enormous stadium through the medium of two little buttons. The first button, by my left elbow, set off a loud gong-like chime with ascending notes, warning the 87,000 or so in the vast Megadome that an announcement would follow. The second button, further to the left, enabled him to tell the multitude: 'Mrs Bruce Robinson, of Ramsey Street, St Kilda, is asked to go to the administration office for a message from her sister'.

For the rest of the match I prevailed on Mr Costin, kind man that he was, to let me be the gong-button pusher to precede his announcements – a sort of modern hi-tech John the Baptist warm-up act – because I loved the feeling of heady power that came with the ability to communicate immediately with 87,000 people at the push of a button. I also knew that ten thousands miles away in Durban my brother was up before daybreak to watch the televised match, and I liked the notion that he could hear my chimes every time Mr Costin had to communicate with the great Australian public. When Mr Costin was out of his chair it was a huge temptation to use the other microphone to announce: 'Will Mrs Stompie Van der Merwe of Bultfontein please come to the administration office to reclaim her husband...' But professionalism won out, and the system went unabused.

I watched that great servant of English cricket, Graham Gooch, plodding in his unathletic-looking way beside Ian Botham to open the England innings, and I was reminded of Alan Ross's description of Tony Lock at the wicket. Ross wrote: "There is

147

a curious turn-of-the-century look about Lock at the wicket. Partly it is the spat-like flaps of his pads, partly his rolled-down sleeves and Edwardian stance..." and you knew at once what he meant. Lock's pads seemed so much wider than those of other batsmen you almost believed they were slatted, as in the 1890s.

Gooch, too, had a turn-of-the century look about him, I decided. That subaltern's moustache from the time of the Boer War would have made Gooch seem at home in a scarlet tunic. And his strange stance also had about it the exaggerations endemic to military postures – the backside thrust out, the knock-knees together and the neck arched at an extreme angle; these could only have come from the orders of some crazed instructor at Sandhurst. Yet what a mighty bat he had wielded since assuming the captaincy! With his high-pitched voice, as well as his scoring consistency, he was carrying on more than one of the traditions of the great W.G. Grace.

In the event England started badly, losing Botham and Stewart caught behind off Wasim Akram and Aqib respectively, though Botham appeared to believe he hadn't touched the ball with the bat. The television replay supported Botham. Gooch and Hick moved things along satisfactorily – though Hick seemed increasingly uncomfortable against the legspinners of Mushtaq. So deeply uncomfortable was he that it was no surprise when Mushtaq had him failing to pick the 'bosie' – the ball darting in to trap him plumb in front with his bat still up in the air.

And when Gooch pulled Mushtaq straight to Aqib at square leg the Pakistanis went

Inzamam-ul-Haq just gets in as Stewart takes off the bails.

wild, knowing that with four wickets down England were starting to look shaky.

Yet there was still considerable batting strength to come, and Fairbrother and Lamb began to put together a sound partnership, keeping the run-rate ahead of that of Pakistan. Things were starting to look good for England at 141 for four. Then suddenly Wasim Akram struck a deadly double-blow, removing Lamb and Lewis in successive balls. Both deliveries were fast and swinging in to smash into the stumps. These were the blows that broke the back of the England batting.

Fairbrother tried bravely, with courageous support from Reeve, but the run-rate was now getting beyond reach. In trying desperately to hit boundaries Fairbrother top-edged a hook to be taken at square-leg by the keeper.

Derek Pringle batted well, hitting the ball much harder than one is accustomed to seeing. He had 18 not out when he ran out of partners. De Freitas was run out for 10 and Illingworth hit out bravely before holing out off Imran for 14. It had been a good rearguard action. But by this time the game was lost. Pakistan emerged worthy winners by 22 runs. They had won their first World Cup.

Many of the team sank to their knees and foreheads in Islamic relief and gratitude, than began to leap for joy about the field, embracing each other as realisation of their victory sank in. It was touching to think how much this achievement would mean to the millions of fans in Pakistan.

Imran and his brilliant young team had fully deserved their win on the day. The world

The moment of triumph: Moin falls to his knees while Imran gestures heavenwards.

The Pakistan team celebrate their victory infront of the crowd at the Melbourne Cricket Ground.

family of cricket was richer for it – much richer than it would have been with a victory for one of the older cricketing countries. Wasim Akram was a deserving Man of the Match. Apart from his quickfire 33 runs, he had taken three key wickets in Botham, Lamb and Lewis. Mushtaq was another hero of the bowling, taking three for 41 in 10 overs, getting Gooch, Hick and Reeve, and Aqib with two for 27 in 10 overs he had helped to close down the English run rate.

So ended this absorbing 39-match series played by nine national teams over nearly five weeks all across Australia and New Zealand. Fireworks exploded in the sky over the Melbourne Cricket Ground as the record one-day crowd of saluted the Pakistanis for winning their last five matches in succession to take the title. It was a staggering thought that the 87,182 were only a small fragment in scale of the multi-million worldwide audience via television.

PAKISTAN	
Aamir Sohail c Stewart b Pringle	4
Ramiz Raja lbw b Pringle	8
*Imran Khan c Illingworth b Botham	72
Javed Miandad c Botham b Illingworth	58
Inzamam-ul-Haq b Pringle	42
Wasim Akram run out	33
Salim Malik not out	0
Extras (lb 19, nb 7)	32
TOTAL (6 wkts, 50 overs, 212 min)	249

Ijaz Ahmed, +Moin Khan, Mushtaq Ahmed and Aqib Javed did not bat.

FALL OF WICKETS: 1-20, 2-24, 3-163, 4-197, 5-249, 6-249

BOWLING: Pringle 10-2-22-3 (nb 5, w 3), Lewis10-2-52-0 (nb 2, w 1), Botham 7-0-42-1 (w 1), DeFreitas 10-1-42-0, Illingworth 10-0-50-1, Reeve 3-0-22-0 (w 1).

ENGLAND	
*GA Gooch c Aqib b Mushtaq	29
IT Botham c Moin b Wasim	0
+AJ Stewart c Moin b Aqib	7
GA Hick lbw b Mushtaq	17
NH Fairbrother c Moin b Aqib	62
AJ Lamb b Wasim	31
CC Lewis b Wasim	0
DA Reeve c Ramiz b Mushtaq1	5
DR Pringle not out	18
PAJ DeFreitas run out	10
RK Illingworth c Ramiz b Imran	14
Extras (lb 5, w 13, nb 6)	24
TOTAL: (49.2 overs, 213 min)	227

FALL OF WICKETS: 1-6, 2-21, 3-59, 4-69, 5-141, 6-141, 7-180, 8-183, 9-208, 10-227

BOWLING: Wasim 10-0-49-3 (nb 4,w 6), Aqib 10-2-27-2 (nb 1, w 3), Mushtaq 10-1-41-3 (w 1), Ijaz 3-0-13-0 (w 2), Imran 6.2-0-43-1 (nb 1), Aamir 10-0-49-0 (w 1)

Umpires: SN Bucknor (West Indies) and BL Aldridge (New Zealand)

Man of the Match: Wasim Akram

PAKISTAN WON BY 22 RUN

Statistics and Averages

QUALIFYING TABLE

	P	W	L	NR	Pts	NRR
New Zealand	8	7	1	0	14	+0.59
England	8	5	2	1	11	+0.47
South Africa	8	5	3	0	10	+0.13
Pakistan	8	4	3	1	9	+0.16
Australia	8	4	4	0	8	+0.20
West Indies	8	4	4	0	8	+0.07
India	8	2	5	1	5	+0.14
Sri Lanka	8	2	5	1	5	-0.68
Zimbabwe	8	1	7	0	2	-1.14

NRR (net run-rate) is the difference between batting and bowling rates. Runs from no-result matches were excluded.

BATTING

(Qualification: 100 runs)

	M	IN	O	Runs	HS	Avge	100	50	Ct/st
M D Crowe (NZ)	9	9	5	456	100*	114.00	1	4	3
P N Kirsten (SA)	8	8	2	410	90	68.33	–	4	2
B M McMillan (SA)	9	5	3	125	33*	62.50	–	–	4
Javed Miandad (Pak)	9	9	2	437	89	62.42	–	5	1
Ramiz Raja (Pak)	8	8	2	349	119*	58.16	2	–	3
N H Fairbrother (Eng)	9	7	2	285	75*	57.00	–	3	6
D C Boon (Aus)	8	8	1	368	100	52.57	2	–	-
A Ranatunga (SL)	8	7	2	262	88*	52.40	–	2	1
B C Lara (WI)	8	8	1	333	88*	47.57	–	4	2
M Azhariddin (Ind)	8	7	0	332	98	47.42	–	4	1
S R Tendulkar (Ind)	8	7	1	283	84	47.16	–	3	2
A H Jones (NZ)	9	9	2	322	78	46.00	–	3	2
K C Wessels (SA)	9	9	2	313	85	44.71	–	3	7
M J Greatbatch (NZ)	7	7	0	313	73	44.71	–	3	4
K R Rutherford (NZ)	9	7	2	212	65*	42.40	–	3	3
D L Haynes (WI)	7	7	1	251	93*	41.83	–	1	4
A Flower (Zim)	8	8	2	146	115*	41.00	1	–	6/1
D M Jones (Aus)	8	8	1	276	90	39.42	–	2	2
K L T Arthurton (WI)	8	7	1	233	58*	38.83	–	2	1
P V Simmons (WI)	4	4	0	153	110	38.25	1	–	1

* Denotes Not out.

BOWLING

(Qualification: 5 wickets)

	O	M	R	W	Avge	Best	5i	Econ
D A Reeve (Eng)	34.4	4	126	8	15.75	3-38	-	3.63
P N Kirsten (SA)	18	1	87	5	17.40	3-31	-	4.83
Wasim Akram (Pak)	89.4	7	338	18	18.77	4-32	-	3.77

U C Hathurusinghe (SL)	17	0	97	5	19.40	4-57	-	5.70
Mushtaq Ahmad (Pak)	78	3	311	16	19.43	3-41	-	3.98
M Prabhakar (Ind)	57.1	5	245	12	20.41	3-41	-	4.28
A C Cummins (WI)	59	1	246	12	20.50	4-33	-	4.16
C Z Harris (NZ)	72.1	4	342	16	21.37	3-15	-	4.73
M R Whitney (Aus)	66	12	260	11	23.88	4-34	-	3.25
W Watson (NZ)	79	11	301	12	25.08	3-37	-	3.81
E A Brandes (Zim)	70.1	7	354	14	25.28	4-21	-	5.04
A A Donald (SA)	78	5	329	13	25.30	3-34	-	4.21
G C Small (Eng)	35	3	127	5	25.40	2-29	-	3.62
A P Kuiper (SA)	41	0	235	9	26.11	3-40	-	5.73
B M McMillan (SA)	73	7	306	11	27.81	3-30	-	4.19
Kapil Dev (Ind)	58	2	251	9	27.88	3-41	-	4.32
P A J DeFreitas (Eng)	85.3	12	319	11	29.00	3-34	-	3.73
G R Larsen (NZ)	76	7	262	9	29.11	3-16	-	3.44
P L Taylor (Aus)	37.4	1	147	5	29.40	2-14	-	3.90
I T Botham (Eng)	89	7	306	16	19.12	4-32	-	3.43

MOST RUNS SCORED

M D Crowe (NZ)	456
Javed Miandad (Pak)	437
P N Kirsten (SA)	410
D C Boon (Aus)	368

MOST HUNDREDS SCORED

D C Boon (Aus)	2
Ramiz Raja (Pak)	2

MOST FIFTIES SCORED

Javed Miandad (Pak)	5
M D Crowe (NZ)	4
P N Kirsten (SA)	4
B C Lara (WI)	4

FASTEST SCORING
(runs per 100 balls; 250 runs)

M D Crowe (NZ)	90.66
M J Greatbatch (NZ)	87.92
S R Tendulkar (Ind)	83.98
B C Lara (WI)	81.62

MOST WICKETS TAKEN

Wasim Akram (Pak)	18
Mushtaq Ahmed (Pak)	16
C Z Harris (NZ)	16
I T Botham (Eng)	16
E A Brandes (Zim)	14

MOST ECONOMICAL BOWLERS
(runs per over; 50 overs bowled)

D N Patel (NZ)	3.10
M R Whitney (Aus)	3.25
D R Pringle (Eng)	3.27
C J McDermott (Aus)	3.37
I T Botham (Eng)	3.43
G R Larsen (NZ)	3.44

MOST NO-BALLS

Wasim Akram (Pak)	22
D R Pringle (Eng)	16

MOST WIDES

Wasim Akram (Pak)	48
A A Donald (SA)	32

MOST DISMISSALS

D J Richardson (SA) (14ct, 1st)	15
Moin Khan (Pak) (1ct, 3st)	14
D Williams (WI) (11ct, 3st)	14
I A Healy (Aus) (9ct)	9
A J Stewart (Eng) (8ct, 1st)	9

MOST CATCHES

K C Wessels (SA)	7
N H Fairbrother (Eng)	6

HIGHEST TOTALS

313-7	**Sri Lanka** v Zimbabwe	New Plymouth
312-4	Sri Lanka v **Zimbabwe**	New Plymouth
280-6	**England** v Sri Lanka	Ballarat
268-8	**West Indies** v Sri Lanka	Berri
265-6	**Australia** v Zimbabwe	Hobart
264-6	**Pakistan** v New Zealand	Auckland

LOWEST TOTALS

74	**Pakistan** v England	Adelaide
125	**England** v Zimbabwe	Albury
134	England v **Zimbabwe**	Albury
136	**West Indies** v South Africa	Christchurch
137	Zimbabwe v **Australia**	Hobart

Epilogue
The Future of World Cricket

Indeed the mighty multitude that watched the final of the World Cup of 1992 at the Melbourne Cricket Ground was only a tiny fraction of the universal audience. According to the media figures, the international viewership, listenership and readership for the World Cup numbered more than a billion in twenty-nine countries all over the world.

So what will be the future for what has clearly become a global game in every sense of the word? What changes will be made in national and international organisation? Which countries will emerge as new challengers?

Pakistan

Pakistan's victory, in retrospect, was the best result from the game's point of view. England, the mother and the inventor of cricket, did not need the propagative results of victory as much as Pakistan did, nor could the joy of English cricket followers have approached, let alone exceeded, the peak of rejoicing that initiated days of celebration in Pakistan over the achievement of Imran Khan and his fellow national heroes.

International heroes too, because they were well worthy of the mantle of victory. Pakistan's cricket peaked in the final – perfect timing for the best occasion. Their cricket was marked throughout the tournament, even before the victories started to amount, by its positive, attacking spirit. Wasim Akram was the leading wicket-taker of the series; Mushtaq Ahmed joint second. And their fastest and most deadly bowler, Waqar Younis, had not even played! As England were to discover in the summer, Pakistan cricket is formidable indeed.

Imran Khan, building a cancer hospital in his country in honour of his mother, found victory in the World Cup of great assistance in his fund-raising, just as the South Africans, in reaching the semi-finals, helped their country in the matter of the referendum.

Australia

On the whole, the Australians took their comparative lack of success, with their own peculiar antipodean brand of stoic fortitude. After all, other previous champions, India and the West Indies had fared worse. But the future of Australian cricket – the source of so many innovations in the last twenty years – was suddenly not so clear. As Neville Oliver comments: "from home-made cedar bats to coloured clothing under lights in a place set up as a prison is a long way to come in two hundred years. Where are we headed next?" In coming years Australian teams may contain more non-English names as the country absorbs thousands of non-English migrants whose children are taking to cricket, but this is unlikely to alter the parochialism that is such a feature of every walk of Australian life. "Western Australians," says Neville Oliver, "see themselves as living in another country with life sadly sometimes interrupted by decisions made 'over East', while residents of Melbourne and Sydney throw taunts about the relative merits of each city with the fervour of Khruschev insulting John Kennedy." As it happens, it was a Tasmanian, David Boon, who emerged from the contest with his reputation most advanced – having scored two fine centuries, a total of 368 runs at an average of 52.57. But for some strange reason Boon had not opened in four crucial matches. Something was amiss with Australian cricket.

India

"The eternal question in Indian cricket," says Mihir Bose, "is 'whither Indian cricket?' As long as I can remember, and I have been following Indian cricket since the early ninteen-fifties, this is the great question of Indian cricket – perhaps Indian life. It is discussed so often in India, after every disastrous tour or series that newspapers should consider putting the headline in permanent type. The continual expectations of victory that Indians sometimes entertain, impose a heavy burden. But part of the enduring charm and magic of Indian cricket is its ability to believe that in the midst of the heaviest downpour the next moment will be diamond-bright and shiny. A nation that can retain such optimism in the face of such appalling odds can sometimes find it is living in a fool's Paradise. But when reality meets expectation, the moment of triumph can be beautifully sweet." Even though India lost five of the eight matches played, comfort could be taken from the strike rate of Kapil Dev (161 runs off 129 balls) and Tendulkar (283 runs off 337 balls) and the performance of the captain, Azharuddin whose average was over 47. The rain cloud over Indian cricket was not likely to be permanent.

New Zealand

Nothing could be said against the state of cricket in New Zealand – not with the astonishing Chris Harris, the astounding Mark Greatbatch and the incomparable Martin Crowe (whose average was 114). They had come back from an indifferent home Test series against England with strategies and with a spirit that helped them to win seven of their first eight World Cup matches, scoring in the process more runs at a faster rate than any other team.

This success cast a wholly new light on the domestic game. Second-string players for their clubs suddenly emerged as world-beaters. As far as New Zealand were concerned, critics accorded them full marks for their remarkable run at this World Cup. For a team based on so few frontline players they had worked miracles, winning all but two of their matches on their home pitches which were uniquely slow. But it was to their credit that they had, after all, suited their batting and bowling to these pitches and had been bold enough to try daring new ideas to upset their opponents, for the most part successfully, as when opening the bowling with slow off-spinner Patel, relying on medium to medium-slow defensive accuracy rather than bowling attack, and concentrating all their attacking ideas at the top of their batting order with players like Greatbatch exploiting the fielding restrictions during the first ten overs to loft the ball over the inner ring.

In another sense, however, one had felt throughout that the New Zealanders would be caught out at some stage, especially if they had to play on quicker pitches, and that sooner or later some vigorous attack would expose the limited dimensions and relative emptiness of their rather bare bowling larder.

But as they had circled the field in Auckland waving their farewells and thanking their supporters, several of the players weeping openly, my thoughts centred less on their limitations as a team than on their amazing performances in spite of those limitations. It had taken batting of rare genius to expose their limitations, and the exposition had come tauntingly late in the contest, snatching the prize of a place in the finals with excruciatingly cruel timing to dash their hopes in the midst of their highest expectations.

If it was any consolation to the New Zealanders, they had shaken the cricket world profoundly and reminded it that in Crowe they were still able to produce players of the highest world class to continue traditions of greatness of the likes of Sutcliffe, Reid, Donnelly, Hadlee, Turner and Dempster.

And yet, as Iain Gallaway explains, the structure of cricket in New Zealand is changing. Pressure has been mounting steadily to shift the control of cricket to the more populous centres of Auckland and Wellington. "The New Zealand Cricket Council was formed in 1894 with headquarters in Christchurch – where it has remained for ninety-eight years. It should celebrate its centennial safely in that city, but how much longer it will remain there is an open question. The executive of the council for decades comprised only Canterbury-based administrators chaired by a Christchurch person. Today it is elected from candidates throughout the country, and, after the retirement of Walter Hadlee, the chairmanship moved immediately North. Probably the only thing which has enabled Christchurch to survive for so long has been the rivalry between the two North Island centres, Wellington and Auckland. Christchurch survives while the 'heavies' jockey for position."

South Africa

When a later history of South African cricket comes to be written it will reflect thee distinct phases of participation, the second of which is not yet complete in 1992, and the third of which has scarcely begun. The three phases will be:

1. Major participation by English-speaking whites;
2. Major participation by Afrikaans-speaking whites;
3. Major participation nationwide by blacks.

The final phase of South African cricket development, the emergence of the black majority to a rightful claim on merit to selection for the national team, has progressed since the South African Cricket Board was launched in November 1977 to re-commit non-racial cricket to the broader struggle for non-racial sport in a non-racial democratic society. It was under the Board that the mainstream of black cricket was led to the point of unity achieved with the white administrators in the 1990's at last to form one consolidated cricket body in South Africa for the first time.

Central to this new-found unity is the drive to make cricket a game for all South Africans, and the township coaching scheme is already producing players of obvious promise as future internationals. Specific names are being mentioned of future stars still in their teens, such as a fast bowler named Walter Masemola, and a left-handed opening batsman named Kenneth Mahuwa – these are among the names to watch in South African teams in four or five years' time.

The success of the South African team in this World Cup, and the nationwide following that built up back in South Africa in consequence, led to the team's cricketing exploits influencing the referendum result on March the seventeenth in which sixty-eight per cent of white South Africans voted to continue the reforms of President F.W. de Klerk to remove all traces of apartheid and institute a democratic constitution. And within a month of the World Cup tour, the South Africans, having preceded the tournament with a short tour of India for three one-day contests, were in the Caribbean for three one-day matches and, historically, the first ever Test Match between the two cricket nations and South Africa's first since 1970.

Although the South Africans did well in the world Cup, they found in their short tours of India and the West Indies that the standard of cricket in these two countries was high indeed. They lost 2-1 to the Indians and 3-0 to the West Indians in the limited-overs contests. But in the Test Match in Barbados they came closer to defeating the West Indians than any other team had in fifty-six years.

Both in India and the West Indies, friendships were built up that augur well for future South African teams abroad.

Just as cricket in the West Indies moved from being represented mostly by whites to being represented mostly by blacks, so the success of current attempts to make cricket in South Africa a sport for all will be measured by the time it takes for most members of a South African team chosen on merit to be black – to reflect at least the racial demographics of the country.

That will be the ultimate sign of success for South African cricket, leaving it free finally to pursue the more normal yardsticks of cricketing success — defeat of opponents.

For cricketers everywhere that will, in liberation terms, be good news.But for South Africa's cricketing opponents, in cricketing terms, it will be bad news indeed!

West Indies

As is the case with India and Australia, it appeared that the failure of the West Indians to impose themselves (as they had in the past) was a temporary set-back. Lara and Cummins, for example, both looked extremely promising. And yet it was clear that the process of rebuilding the team around the new leader, Richie Richardson, was far from complete. Hugh Crosskill comments: "the fact that another 'small islander' has assumed the mantle of captaincy bears out the prediction made over thirty years ago by the late Sir Frank Worrell that players from the Leeward and Windward Islands would eventually form the foundation upon which West Indies cricket is built. But there could be difficult and contentious times ahead. The entire regional integration movement, wonderfully illustrated by West Indian cricket, is under intense pressure from global developments in trade and investment. Fresh differences in approach and direction are beginning to surface among the nations of the English-speaking Caribbeans. If West Indies cricket is to avoid a return to the insularity of the early days, the administrators will have to step up efforts to ensure that it remains in step with the political, social and economic developments taking place beyond the boundary."

Sri Lanka

The future of Sri Lankan cricket is, in many ways, emblematic of the future of cricket in the world at large. The Sri Lankans reminded us at Basin Reserve in Wellington that they are always capable of springing surprises. They restricted South Africa to 195 in fifty overs and then, with Mahanama 68 and Ranatunga 64, beat their rivals by three wickets. Bandula Warnapura, the man who led Sri Lanka in their first official Test in February 1982 claims that "the kind of cricket we play is more suited to one day cricket. Most of the club matches are played for two days and everybody is in a rush to finish the innings and to score a win". And as testimony to this thesis he cites Sri Lanka's 2-1 victory in the one-day home series against Australia played in August 1992.

Yet somewhere something is lacking in Sri Lankan cricket. Warnapura explains, "we lack the finish, we lack the fighting qualities, we lack professionalism in our cricket. These are three factors we have to address. When you talk about technique or the talent, we have got these but what we need to be equal to all other Test playing countries is mentality of psychology. I think we have still got to develop ourselves into a winning team."

"From the player's point of view," remarks Vijay Rana, "the most discouraging aspect of Sri Lankan cricket is the infighting among the members of the cricket board. There is often a rebel group, sometimes supported by ambitious government ministers who are themselves vying for position, attempting to displace the current board. Elections for the posts of president and secretary of the board are held every year. According to a government law passed in 1974, no individual can hold these posts for more than two years. However, instead of bringing stability to the sport, this ruling has encouraged more infighting. Board elections are like mini parliamentary elections, with candidates sending out printed brochures extolling their qualifications, to about a hundred clubs and district associations. 'These changes do make our cricketers jittery ... they just wonder how they will be treated. 'It is like having a different employer every year', complained Chandra Schaffter, who was once Sri Lanka's opening bowler and who came to England in 1991 as manager of the Test team."

The system means that experience and talented players are thrown out of the Sri Lankan team and favoured players brought in. "The most glaring example of this," says Vijay Rana, "was the retirement of the hero of the 1984 Lords' Test, Sidath Wettimuny, who scored a sparkling 190 runs. The dismissal of Captain Arjuna Ranatunga who was accused by the manager, Stanley Jayasinghe of displaying a "haughty" attitude and "double standards" after their tour to New Zealand during 1990-91, was even raised in parliament, and the accusations aired that Ranatunga had had to pay the price of his father belonging to the opposition Sri Lanka Freedom Party. Bandula Warnapura, Sri Lanka's captain in the first official Test match, conceded that changing captain for almost every tour adversely affected the cohesion of the team."

But Vijay Rana tells, also, of the movements working to improve the future of cricket in his country. "The Sri Lankan Cricket Foundation was formed in 1981 to promote young talents by organising competitive cricket for the under 17s and under-19s. Experienced cricket coaches such as Les Lenham, Peter Philpott and Sir Garfield Sobers have been invited to sharpen the technique of the young players."

Scarred by political violence and ethnic hatred in the past, Sri Lankan cricket is to enter a new era of revival. The financial future of Sri Lankan cricket looks secure for the coming years. In the next twelve months, Sri Lankans will witness a greater participation of their country in international cricket than there has ever been since their entry into the charmed International circuit in February 1982.

Zimbabwe

There had been no early heroics this time and their progression had been pretty dismal until that last astonishing match against the favourites, England. "Where now?" asks Bob Nixon:

> Will Zimbabwe have to win the ICC trophy for the fourth time in succession to qualify for the next World Cup? Will young African players using all the facilities and coaches of the former whites-only high schools emerge as real contenders for places in the national sides? It is twelve years since the schools and clubs were opened to all races. Will Zimbabwe return to compete in South African competitions now that South Africa is once more welcome in all the cricketing countries? And most important will Zimbabwe be able to hold on to young players before they look for the chance to play Test cricket elsewhere? The financial rewards for players in Zimbabwe are poor. To a large extent, they have to move away if they wish to make a career of cricket. With so few good cricketers Zimbabwe simply cannot afford to lose any players if they are to make any impact on the international scene.

The challenge for Zimbabwe would seem to be to establish their own first-class structure and to offer their young players the certainty of international competition. The one is almost certainly, dependent on the other.

Other Countries?

Will future World Cups be played out between teams other than those who competed in 1992? Ralph Dellor has a number of suggestions:

> Bermuda has a strong cricketing history which dates back to 1844 when the Garrison lost to an Army XI by three wickets. Domestic competiton has been keen and Bermuda has been the venue for tours from Canada and the United States, several West Indian sides, and touring Test teams on their way to or from the West Indies. In fact, the match between Bermuda and New Zealand at Hamilton in 1972 was recognised as being of first-class status.
>
> The peak of Bermuda's achievement in international cricket came in 1982 when the team reached the final of the ICC Trophy. On the way they beat Malaysia by the little matter of 284 runs — surely a record for sixty-overs cricket. In the final they lost an excellent contest against Zimbabwe by five wickets. It was fitting that Bermuda should have made such an impact in the tournament, for it was their representative on the ICC, Alma Hunt, who first proposed the competition.

While Bermuda, the United States and Canada compete in the Atlantic Tournament in the north, the venue for the South Atlantic Championship is the outcrop of volcanic rock called

Tristan da Cunha. "There might only be two teams and no grass pitch," says Ralph Dellor, " but rivalry is fierce. Many other islands and island groups support keen cricketing activity, right down to the Falklands. The climate there might not be ideal to encourage the growth of the game, but the large influx of British troops since 1982 has ensured that cricket has once again established itself in the islands."

South America might not come to mind as a cricketing centre, with no British possessions other than Belize. And yet, as Ralph Dellor reminds us "it is the other aspect of English influence – commerce – which planted the game in that continent. Bearing in mind the participants in the Falklands conflict, it is ironic that the strongest cricketing country in South America has been Argentina, mainly because of the large British contingent involved with the railway and meat-packing industries. Argentina had sent teams to England on numerous occasions – playing even against the MCC at Lord's. Argentina has been represented in the ICC Trophy – but so far without any conspicuous success."

Across the South Atlantic in Africa, cricket is played, as Ralph Dellor points out, "on a wider scale. Apart from in the major cricket-playing nations, the game can be found across most of the continent which has had exposure to British rule. East Africa, consisting of Kenya, Uganda and Tanzania came together in 1960 as the East African Cricket Conference, admitted to the ICC as an associate member in 1966. The body was expanded to include Zambia in 1968, and Malawi in 1966. By then, East Africa had taken part in two ICC competitions. In 1990 Kenya reached the semi-final."

Regular appearances in the ICC Trophy has also been a feature of some of the smaller nations of Asia. "For many years," says Ralph Dellor, "Bangladesh's cricket, what little there was of it, was inextricably tied up with that of India and Pakistan, and after Independence in 1973 its facilities fell into decline. Then, however, the government stepped in to redevelop the game. By 1979 Bangladesh was taking part in the ICC Trophy reaching the semi-finals in 1983 and 1990."

Malaysia, Hong Kong and Singapore have also featured in the ICC Trophy competitions, as Ralph Dellor tells it, "with boundless enthusiasm but limited success. Nepal became an affiliate member in 1988. Fiji and Papua New Guinea are two of the stronger cricketing centres in the Pacific Basin. Papua New Guinea (where cricket was introduced at the turn of the century as an alternative activity to head-hunting) claimed some impressive scalps on their way to the ICC semi-final in 1982."

The major cricketing powers on Continental Europe are undoubtedly Holland and Denmark. There have, according to Ralph Dellor, "been suggestion that these two countries could take part in one-day competitions played by the English first-class counties. Their record in the ICC Trophy speaks for itself. Denmark reached the semi-finals in 1979; Holland the finals in 1990. Some three thousand players regularly take part in the game in both countries – and the game is growing in popularity."

COULD THE WORLD CUP FORMAT BE IMPROVED?

There is general agreement that the rain-delay rules (to put it mildly) leave much to be desired ... Perhaps the enterprising entrepreneurial ways of W.G.Grace and his contemporaries could be brought to bear on future tournaments.

In W.G.'s day regional rivalries on a greater than local scale made for cricket of wider significance – North v. South, for instance.

If the 1992 World Cup had ended with a match between Northern Hemisphere and Southern Hemisphere, some interesting global arguments could have been settled. Perhaps the line-ups would have been:

Northern Hemisphere	Southern Hemisphere
Batting:	
Gooch (England)	Wessels (South Africa)
Lara (West Indies)	Boon (Australia)
Botham (England)	Moody (Australia)
Richardson (West Indies)	Crowe (c) (New Zealand)
Tendulkar (India)	Kirsten (South Africa)
Ul-Haq (Pakistan)	Jones (Australia)
Imran Khan (c) (Pakistan)	Waugh (Australia)
Kapil Dev (India)	Kuiper (South Africa)
Ambrose (West Indies)	McMillan (South Africa)
Tillekeratne (wkt) (Sri Lanka)	Smith (wkt) (New Zealand)
Mushtaq Ahmed (Pakistan)	Donald (South Africa)
Bowling:	
Ambrose	Donald
Imran Khan	McMillan
Kapil Dev	Waugh
Botham	Kuiper
Tendulkar	Kirsten
Mushtaq Ahmed	Moody

And if, on conclusion of this match, the World Cup committee could have borrowed an American idea and awarded the honours of selection to a World Cup XI, this could have been a fitting salute to the best of the cricketers on this global cricket stage. For my part, I prefer to show the youthful vigour of the great old game by selecting a final team only from among those players 25 years of age or younger at the start of the 1992 World Cup tournament, to illustrate what an exciting future lies ahead:

Brian Lara, age 22, West Indies
Andrew Hudson, age 25, South Africa
Graeme Hick, age 25, England
Sachin Tendulkar, age 18, India
Inzamam Ul-Haq, age 22, Pakistan
Hansie Cronje, age 22, South Africa
Jonty Rhodes, age 22, South Africa
Chris Lewis, age 24, England
Wasim Akram, age 25, Pakistan
Mushtaq Ahmed, age 21, Pakistan
Hashan Tillekeratne, age 24, Sri Lanka

Bowling: Wasim Akram, Lewis, Tendulkar, Mushtaq, Cronje, Hick.

And how many will grow to greatness, to challenge the primacy of the likes of Hobbs of England, Gavaskar of India, Trumper and Bradman of Australia, Grace and Hammond of England, Sobers of West Indies, Cameron of South Africa, Larwood of England, Abdul Qadir of Pakistan and Sir Richard Hadlee of New Zealand? And who, studying the diverse origins of these all-time greats and these young stars of the future alike, can doubt the universality of a sport that draws together so many people from so many countries and continents? It is indeed a sport for all regions. It is a genuine World Sport – or more: a Global Game.